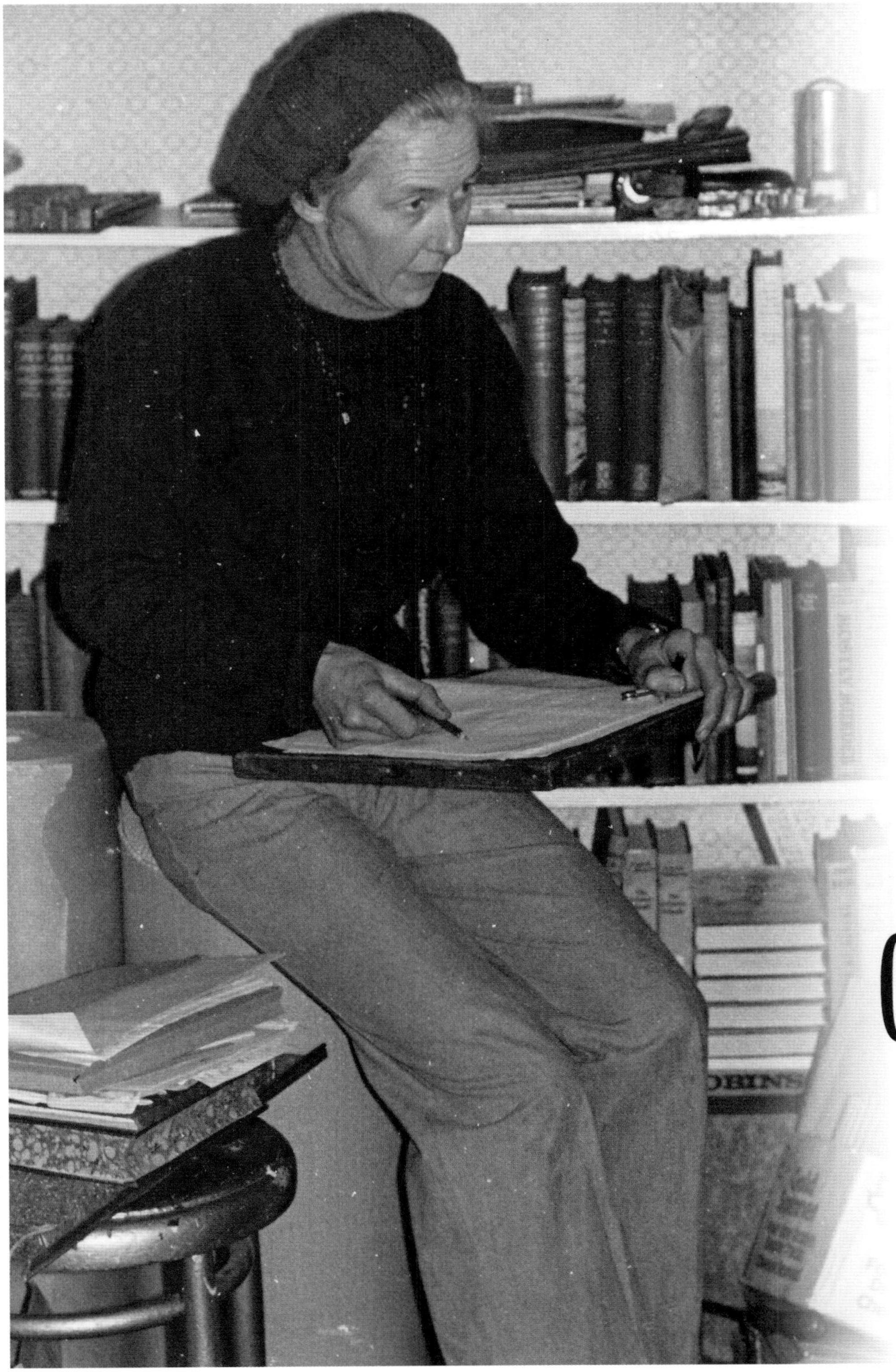

Inside & Out

the art of

Christian Small

Published in the UK by Scotland Street Press,
Edinburgh, 2019

Originally published by Lyne Press, 2018

ISBN 978-1-910895-36-8

Design by Simon Fraser

Printed and bound by Books and Catalogues, Poland

The poem Rose Stalks in Snow was previously published in QUINES: Poems in tribute to Women of Scotland by Gerda Stevenson, Luath Press.

Thanks

to Dr Jamie Reid Baxter for generous assistance;

also to friends and family of Christian Small: Virginia Barnes, John Savory, Chris Atkinson, Gerda Stevenson, Archie Hunter, Susan White-Oakes, the Alice Hamilton Trust; Jim Pratt (photography); Jenny Alldridge, Lucille McLaughlin, Ewan, David, Alison and Roger Small; Andrew Restall; the owners of Christian's art for their kind cooperation.

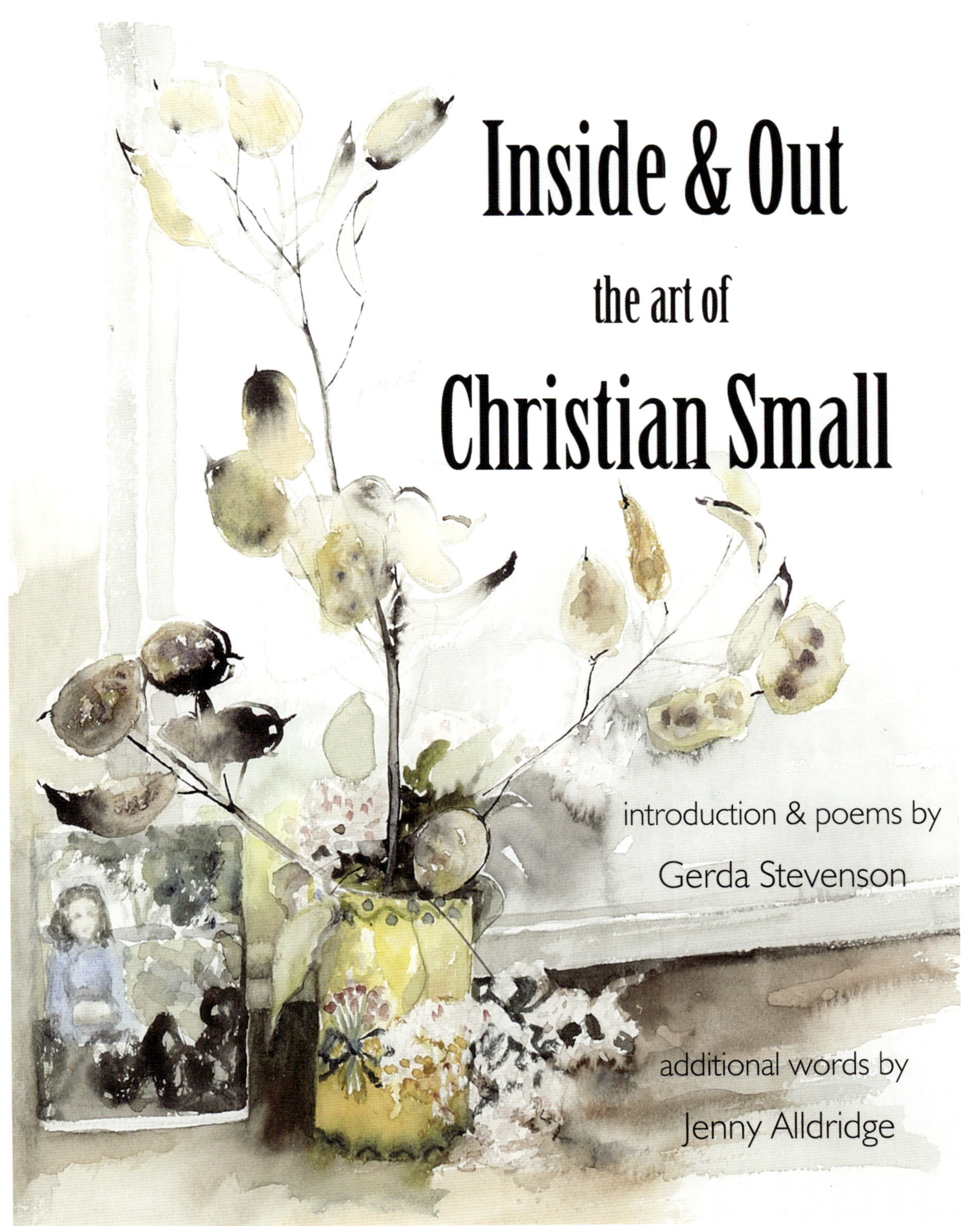

Inside & Out

the art of

Christian Small

introduction & poems by

Gerda Stevenson

additional words by

Jenny Alldridge

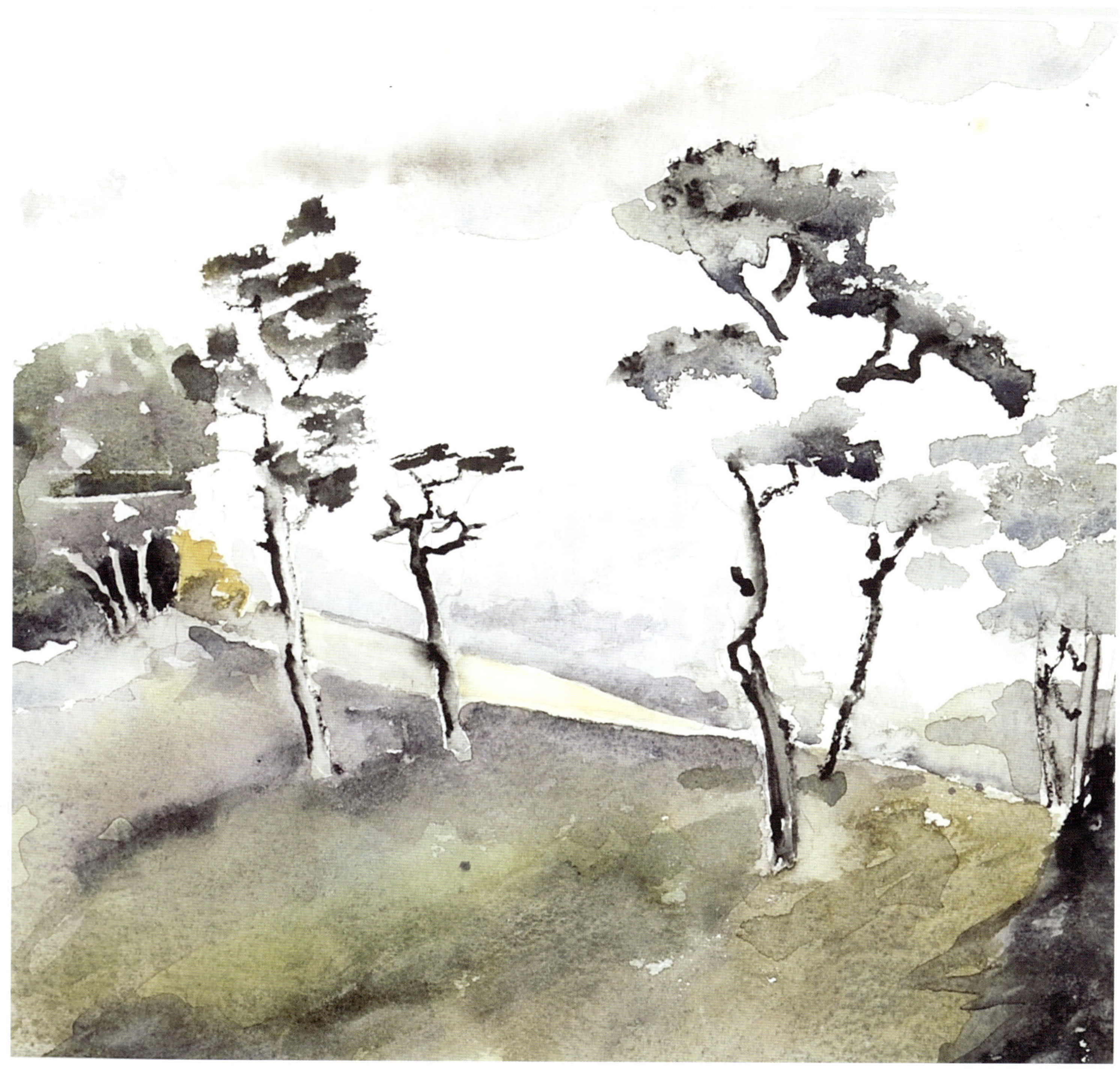

watercolour 230 x 250mm

INTRODUCTION

Christian Small lived in the Scottish Borders village of West Linton for over sixty years. When she died in 2016, aged 90, her family and friends discovered that many people, over several decades, had acquired her paintings. Virginia Barnes, along with other local admirers of Christian's art, gathered these works from their various owners, and organised an exhibition in West Linton Visitor Centre. The result was something of a revelation. We all began to truly appreciate not just the remarkable quality and range, but also the astonishing quantity of the artist's work, in many different media – pencil, charcoal, pen and ink, water colour, and, from her later years, a series of exquisite, masterly collages, using fragments of coloured tissue paper, cardboard and newspaper.

Sculptor Susan White-Oakes comments: *I have always thought of Christian's art as being exceptional. Her choice of subjects was wonderfully imaginative. Pears on a window sash, an armchair with slippers, her paint box - all so evocative of her life. Her landscapes were drawn from around West Linton, their colour and draftsmanship brilliantly capturing aspects of the countryside I know so well - the wind-bent trees, pale green grasses, the rolling Pentland Hills. Her sense of colour was subtle and true to nature, a very difficult thing to achieve. Her drawings too were all outstanding, whether people or still life. It is very unfashionable these days to believe that drawing is a fundamental skill that artists should master. Christian*

Small definitely possessed the ability to draw well, indeed beautifully, be it with pencil, charcoal, crayon or paint brush. Memorable drawings for me are the head of Samuel Becket (taken from a photograph) and the profile of a woman's head, with earring and necklace. Many fellow students on art courses with Christian have remarked to me on her flair and speed of working. This talent enabled her to capture very quickly the essence of the artistic task before her, whatever the medium she was working in.

Andrew Restall, artist and former Head of Visual Communications at Edinburgh College of Art writes: *Here we have someone who set about recording the world she clearly loved - domestic, rural, sometimes intimate, sometimes far, always refreshingly free from pretension or overwork, and thus always immediately accessible. Her hand followed her eye, and from the simplest of economic means to the most full-bodied and complex, she found the appropriate way, never overworked or laborious, with a natural eloquence in the use of the tricky medium of watercolour, enabling the viewer to 'enter' the image and share the vision.*

Due to limitation of space, the exhibition in West Linton Visitor Centre revealed only a fraction of the artist's output. Nevertheless, it was very popular, with a constant flow of visitors throughout that one weekend. A dedicated group emerged, calling itself the Friends and Family of Christian Small, with the aim of producing a book. People were

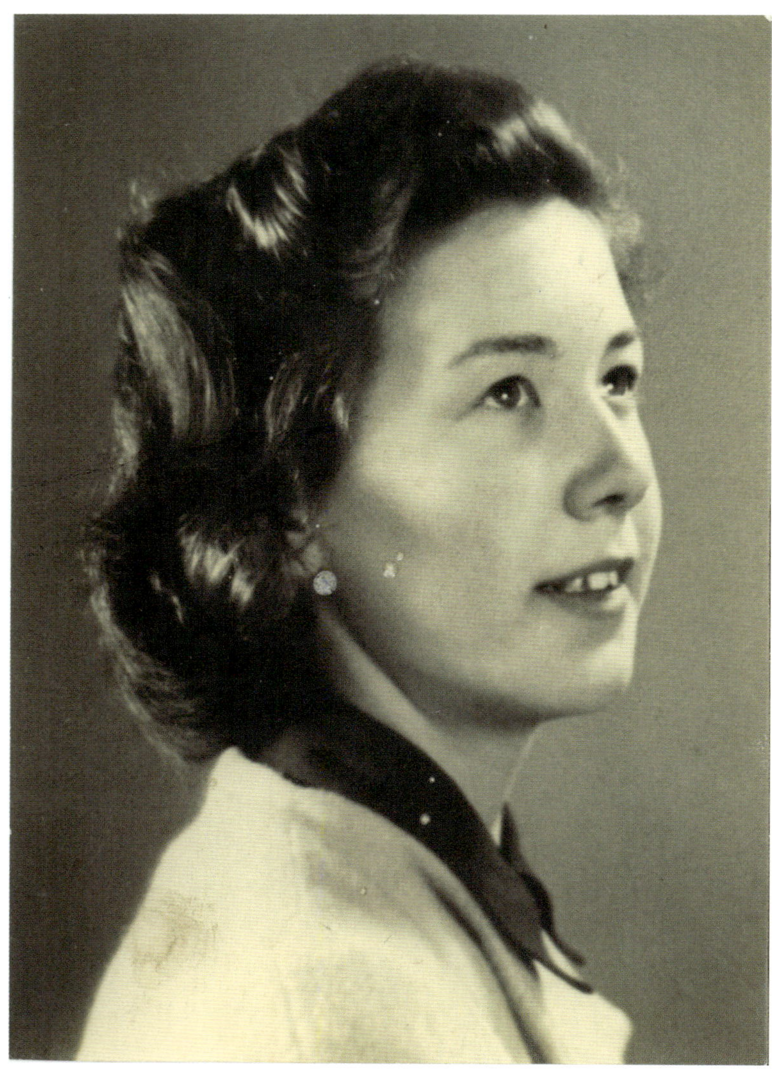

contacted again, and asked to return to the centre with the paintings, and many brought work we hadn't seen before. Jim Pratt set up his lights and camera equipment, and heroically photographed over 200 of Christian's art works in a single day. I was invited to respond to those of my choice by writing a series of poems to be included in the book, and to research and write an introduction. This has been a most pleasurable, intimate experience, and a great privilege. Gradually, the book's shape has emerged, with Christian's daughter Jenny writing prose in her mother's voice, adding an unusually tender layer of insight.

***

The first painting I ever bought was 'a Christian Small'. A glorious riot of dandelions in vivid yellow and green. A teenager at the time, waitressing at weekends in a local restaurant, I proudly offered Christian a fiver from my earnings. She refused. But I insisted, and reluctantly she accepted. Decades on, those wild weeds are framed above my fireplace. Gold-dust to me.

I can't remember not knowing Christian. From early childhood, I've been a close friend of her daughter Jenny. Our mothers had become friendly, having moved to the Scottish Borders village of West Linton around the same time, in the early 50s.

With her family of five children, Christian's household at Yarrow Cottage – two up and two down – was jam-packed. Eventually an extension was built, providing the family with a social area, but until then, the downstairs sitting room doubled as the parental bedroom. Occasionally, Christian would invite me into this intimate space, with its welcoming open fire. I recall her sitting up in bed, reading. I would have been around twelve at the time. I was keen on drawing, painting and sewing, and admired Christian's colourful patchwork quilt. She told me she'd made it from remnants of her children's old clothes. Each patch held a memory for her, she said. She wouldn't have used the word 'precious' or 'treasured' – Christian was rigorously unsentimental - inhibited, even, when it came to emotion. Although she was absolutely fascinated by other people's lives – always deeply interested in weighing up human desires and contradictions in others – she very rarely gave away anything of herself. Yet part of her appeal was her intensity. Incapable of engaging in trivial chit-chat, she loved to talk ideas with people of any age-group – art, literature, ecology, and politics. A girl on the verge of womanhood, I found it exhilarating to be treated as an equal in this way by an older woman.

I think I was always aware that Christian was a conundrum. In one sense, her family experienced a lot of freedom in their early years, spending much of their time out of doors. As my own mother put it, "Christian's children grew up like wild flowers". Any indoor, rainy day ploys that Jenny and I engaged in, such as puppet and dress making, would take place in my home. I don't recall Christian facilitating activities involving her children's friends – her husband Hugh did that. A tense man at home, he was much more relaxed on sprees with a group of children in tow, and one summer, took Jenny, her brother Ewan, and me, on a wonderfully memorable holiday to Norway.

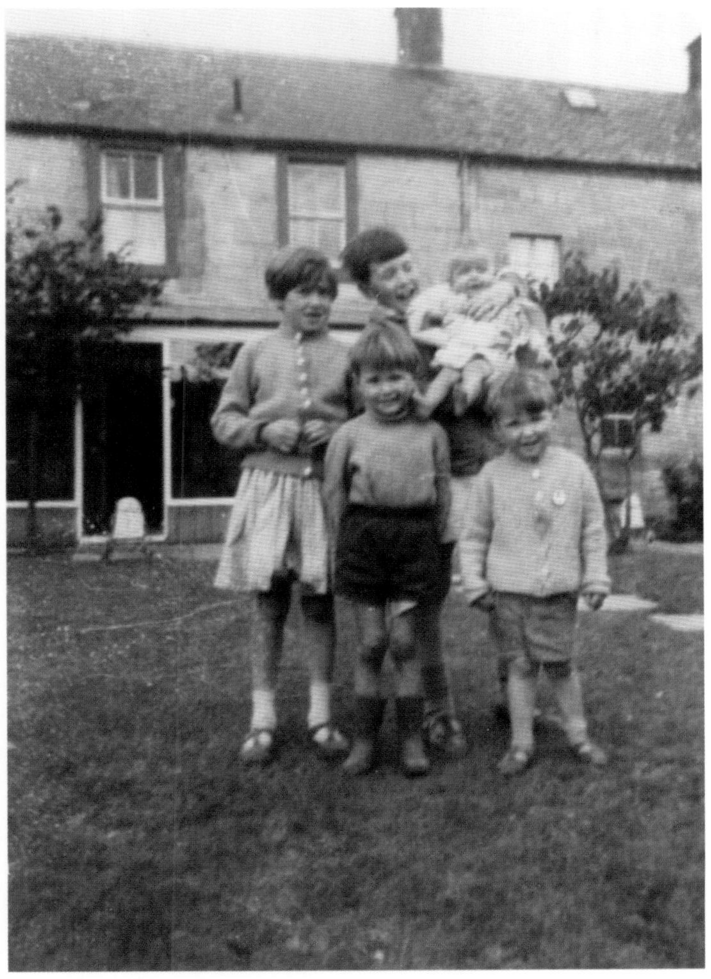

Jenny, Peter holding Roger, Ewan and David in Yarrow Cottage garden, 1964

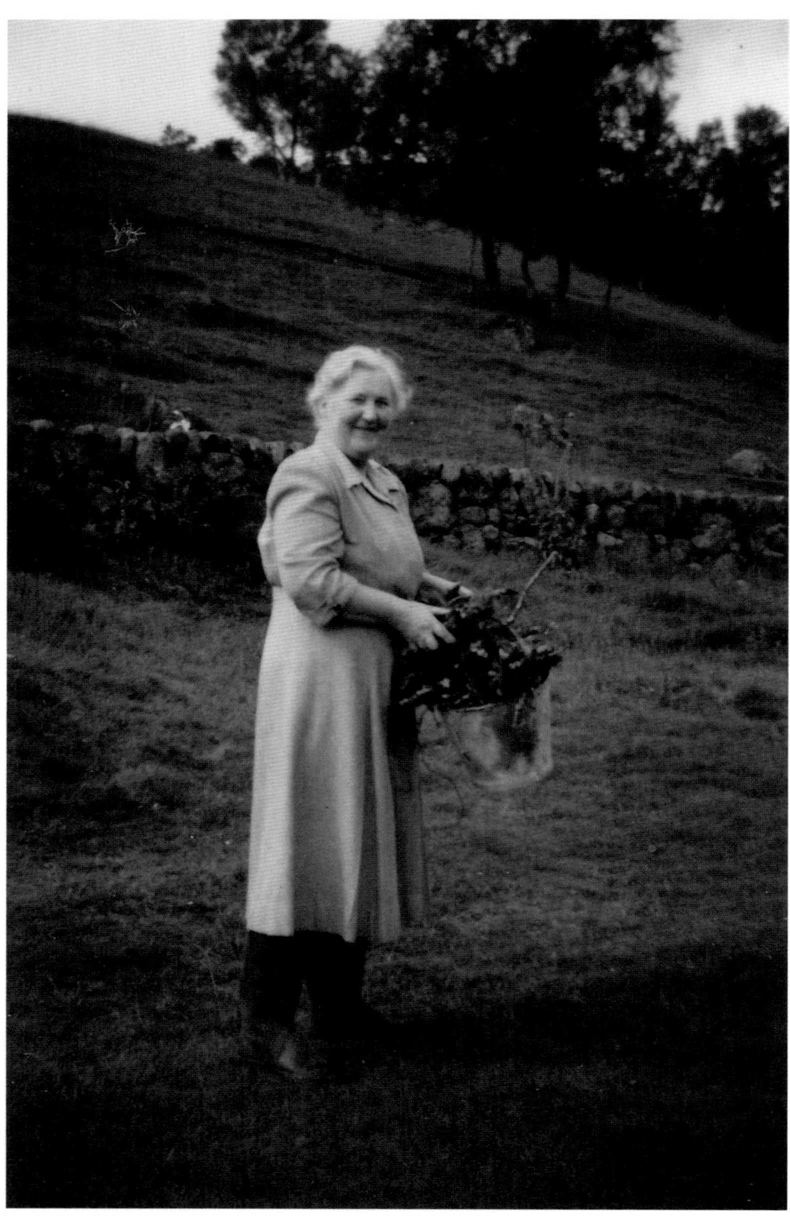

Christian's mother, Christian McCririck, in Glenshee

The family's two grandmothers both lived in the village. Hugh's mother, whom we called Crail Granny, was strict. However, she possessed the unrivalled attraction of a television. Neither Yarrow Cottage nor my own family home had a TV – both Christian and my father being highly suspicious of such an influence. I was prepared to endure the discomfort of Crail Granny's formality for the sake of *Top of the Pops* and *Doctor Who*.

Christian's mother, known as Edinburgh Granny, was a light-hearted, generously nurturing woman. Although she and Christian saw little of one another, this lovely elderly lady regularly invited Jenny and me to tea in Chestnut Cottage, where she'd play board and card games with us. Her exquisite, yet cosy home was full of family photographs and fascinating objects. I remember two in particular – an ornamental scarab beetle from Egypt, made of turquoise stone and brass, and a beautiful china doll called Esme. Also housed in this tiny cottage, were a few items of fine Edwardian furniture, quietly proclaiming a former setting of more genteel status. Christian's father had been a doctor, and I remember the large medical cabinet of polished mahogany and gleaming glass, which once stood, so I was told, in his Dundee surgery.

Growing up in a world managed by adults, children pick up on signs of human interaction without the experience to fully interpret their meaning. Childhood for us was idyllic – paddling in the burn, picnicking in the woods. We weren't intent on understanding our parents' hinterlands. It's only later in life, through sharing conversations and memories, as I've done with Christian's family and friends since her death, that those fragments of knowledge and understanding begin to form a less blurred picture.

***

Christian was born in the city of Dundee, in 1925, to Christian Reid McCririck and Sidney Rintoul. Her older sister Catriona (known as Catrine) had arrived three years earlier. The girls were raised in Dundee, where Sidney established his own GP practice. As a newly qualified doctor, he had served as a Medical Officer in Gallipoli, and then in Mesopotamia, where he was awarded the Military Cross. In the University of St Andrews Roll of Honour and Roll of Service 1914–1919, we read that *Captain Rintoul has shown an absolute disregard for personal danger, and his skill and energy in tending the wounded during the operations round Kirkuk in April and May 1918, under difficult circumstances, were beyond all praise.* The trauma of war returned to haunt Sidney over the years. He struggled with mental health, which nowadays would be diagnosed as Post Traumatic Stress Disorder, suffered by so many war veterans. These days, support for such illness is still patchy, but a century ago it was non-existent. As a GP, Christian's suicidal father had access to drugs. He self-medicated, and battled with addiction, while striving to maintain a respectable medical practice and support his family against the odds.

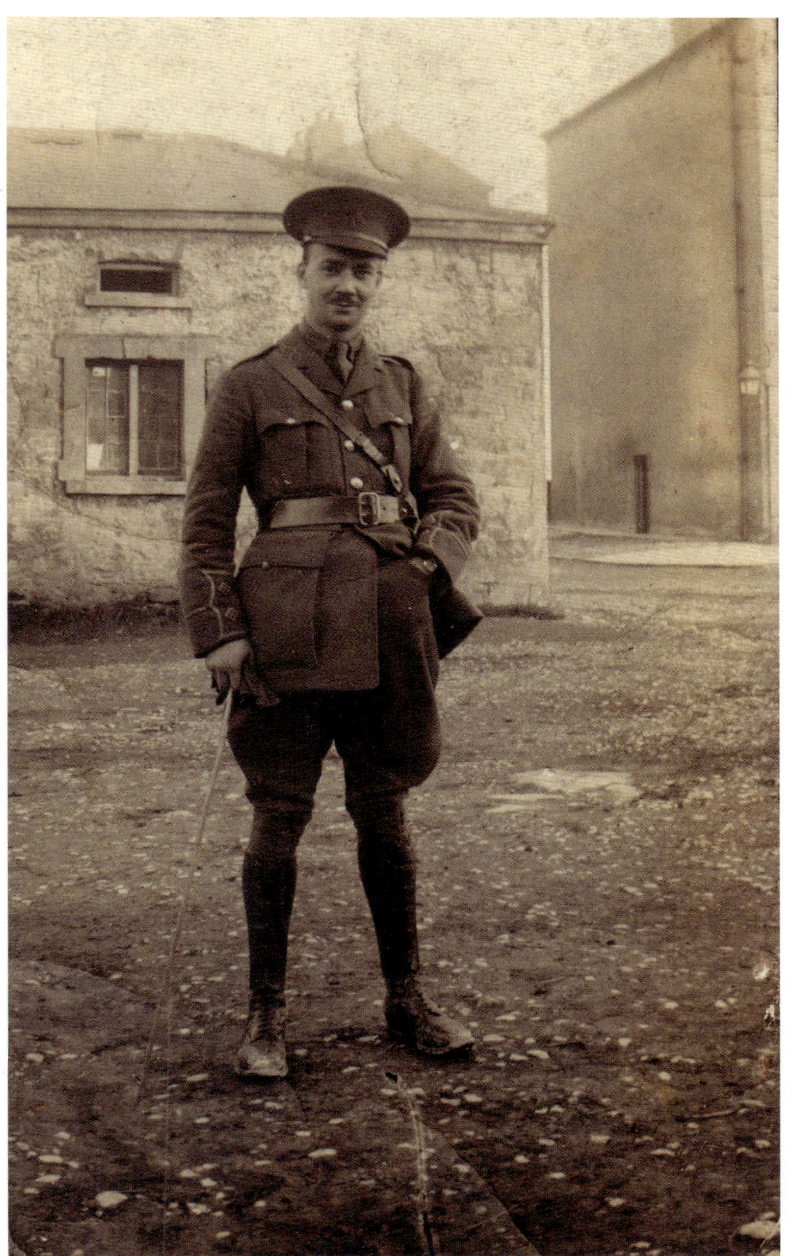

Christian's father, Sidney Rintoul

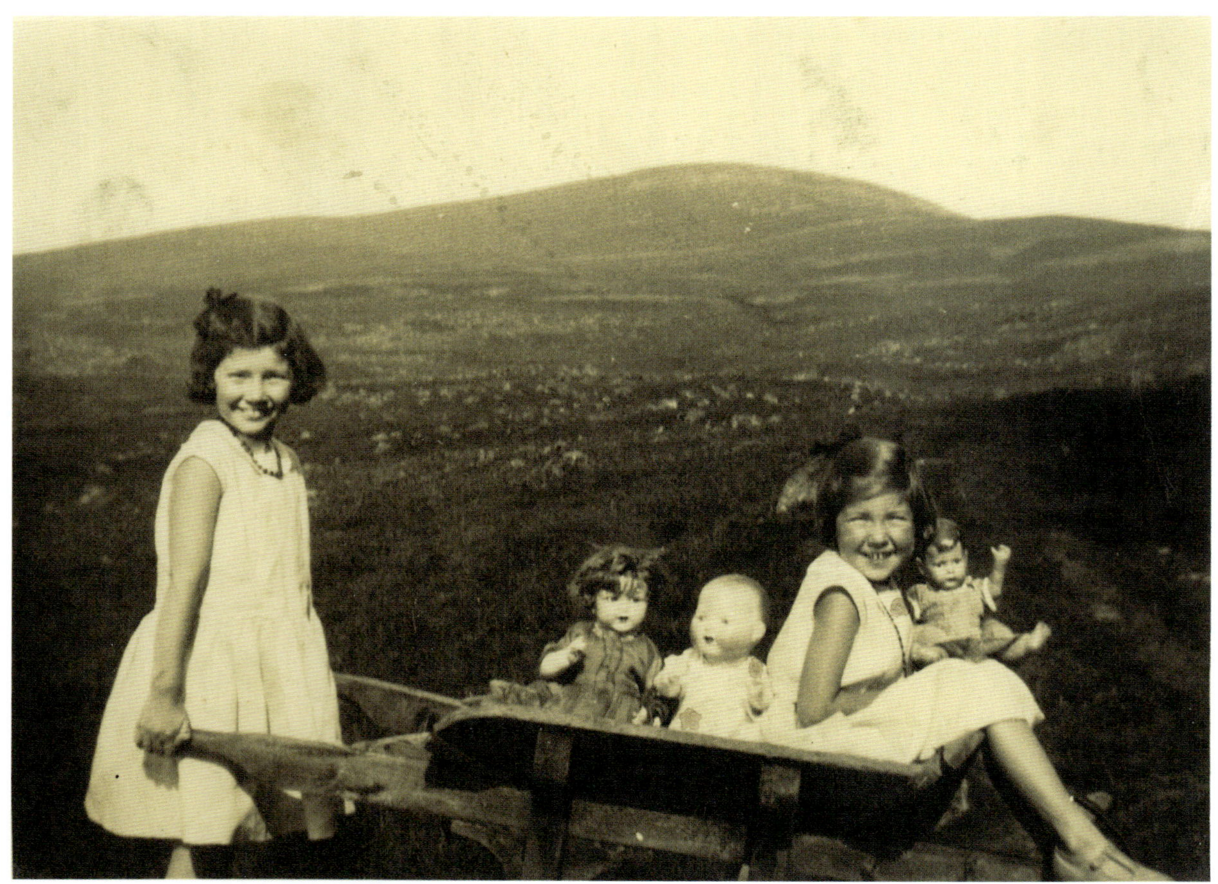

Catrine and Christian (in the wheelbarrow) in Glenshee

Summers were spent in a rented cottage in Glenshee with the maternal grandmother – times of great freedom for the young sisters, and the start of a long love affair Christian had with that part of the Highlands.

The girls were educated at different high schools. Catrine attended Seymour Lodge School, which was relocated from Dundee to Crieff in 1939, and Christian went to Dundee High School. When war broke out, Catrine joined the WRNS. Christian longed to leave home. According to her easy-going sister, Christian always reacted against the restraints and respectability of her upbringing. But at fourteen, she wasn't old enough to follow in her older sister's footsteps. Life must have been stressful at this stage, at home alone with her parents, her father suffering from a frightening and unpredictable illness. She threw herself into her studies, choosing science as her main subject, and excelled academically. She was also good at sport, playing tennis and hockey in the school teams. A sixth-form classmate penned a rhyme about her in the school magazine:

> *Mix caprice, sense of fun, two long legs in a pool;*
> *give them a stir – and you've Christian Rintoul!*

She worked as a Land Girl between leaving school and starting at St Andrews University, where she studied Chemistry, graduating with honours in 1948.

***

Hugh Small was an only child of colonial parents. As a younger boy, he'd been sent home to board at George Watsons in Edinburgh, while his parents were in Sri Lanka and Uganda. But he then briefly attended Dundee High School, where he had a cousin who happened to be in Christian's class. This girl's family owned a holiday house in Glenshee, and these connections brought Christian and Hugh together during their teens. Hugh left school early and joined the merchant navy close to the end of war. His troop ship was bombed and sunk in the Gulf of Aden, off the coast of Africa. Although still only a teenager, as Senior

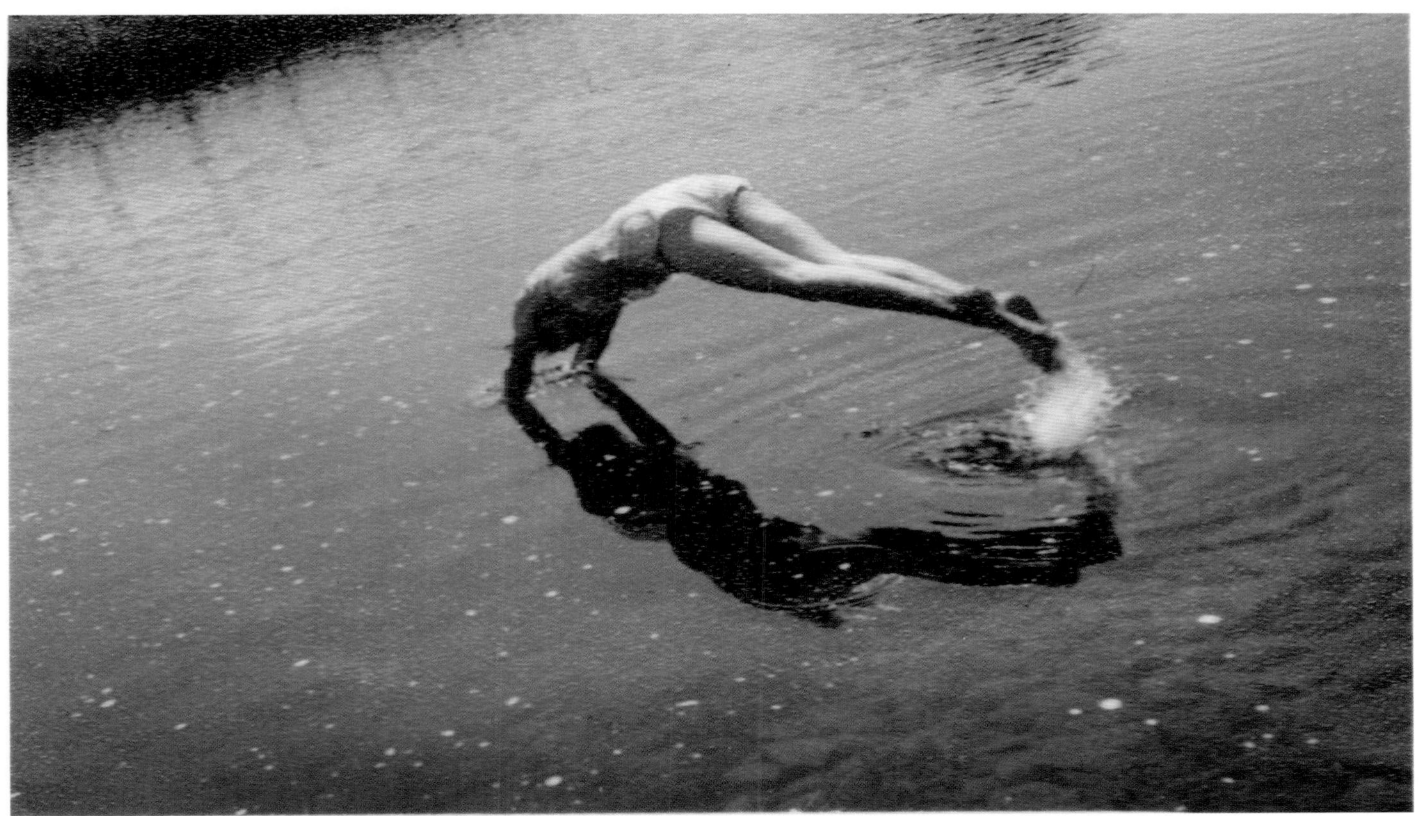

"...two long legs in a pool"

Service, young Hugh was in charge of his lifeboat of men. Without loss of life, this small vessel was rescued by a whaler, and made the long journey to safety in South Africa. A period of recovery followed for Hugh. At the end of the war, he returned to Dundee to study architecture, and at this point, re-established contact with Christian, the two going on a camping holiday to France with another couple.

Employment for Christian after graduation was not straightforward. She applied for a post with Christian Salvesen, a company which had strong Edinburgh connections, including philanthropic initiatives for injured and retired army veterans. Initially, the company was interested in the possibility of taking on this excellent graduate, until they discovered they were dealing with a woman. Christian received a letter of rejection, with the unforgettable words: *We regret your sex.* According to the company, a woman working alongside men was wholly inappropriate, and could not be accommodated. Her first employment took her south to Epsom, where she worked for a laboratory, carrying out experiments on animals. This job didn't last long – she hated it, and returned to Scotland, marrying Hugh in 1950. By this time, her father's mental health had seriously deteriorated. He was now in Gartnavel Royal Hospital, and died soon after. Christian's mother took a position as a Housemistress at Glenalmond College, working there until she retired. Catrine married and settled in the South of England.

Christian and Hugh moved to Edinburgh, where she trained as a primary teacher at Moray House. However, motherhood intervened – five children in ten years, four boys and one girl: Peter, Jenny, Ewan, David and Roger. Christian didn't pursue a career in teaching. The couple moved to Yarrow Cottage in West Linton in 1953. Christian's generation of women was only just emerging from the stifling effects of the infamous Marriage Bar – lifted in 1945 – which prevented professional women from working once they married. Although no longer current, it took many decades for the culture to change. After a brief period of new-found freedom in war-time, due to the need for all hands on deck, women were once again firmly relegated to the narrow parameters of the family home. Although a creative seamstress and knitter, Christian was certainly no domestic goddess. And five young children was quite a handful.

Jenny writes: *Mum didn't work as we grew up. She did a brief spell of supply teaching at Dunsyre in the '70s, then worked in Edinburgh, at Romanes and Paterson on Princes Street, eventually finding permanent employment for many years at the Camera Obscura (next to Edinburgh Castle), which she loved. I remember her painting sometimes, but had no idea about the consuming passion it would become.*

Three ghosts haunted Mum: her father's illness, her unsuccessful marriage and her estrangement from my brother Peter. She was totally uncommunicative about her past and chose not to keep in touch with many of her childhood friends and most members of her extended family. This way she could avoid reminiscing. So we four siblings are left to piece together a jigsaw of fact and conjecture. However, an undeniable energy, eccentricity and creativity that we all agree upon shone through.

Christian's son Ewan remembers: … *a very free childhood. We could walk up the river to Lynedale to have a picnic or just* to play in the water, or explore the Cat Walk above the Lyne. We often went to the old Roman Bridge over Westwater and loved exploring the woods and river there. All these places, trees and water would appear in Christian's paintings and drawings. She drew very deeply on the landscape around West Linton for her work, a landscape that she had walked over many times.

And Jenny again: *She was a member of the Labour Party, joined CND, and went on marches in the '70s. She loved* classical music, *and I remember a grim, unhappy phase when she listened to endless Wagner and Mahler.*

Mum was unable to hide her social awkwardness. Her behaviour was at times rude and abrupt. This caused us much embarrassment over the years, but her friends assure us that this was part of her unique personality. She hated respectability, conformity and authority, and so did Dad. She didn't appear to be close to her own mother, and it was us grandchildren who spent time with Granny, and had to keep

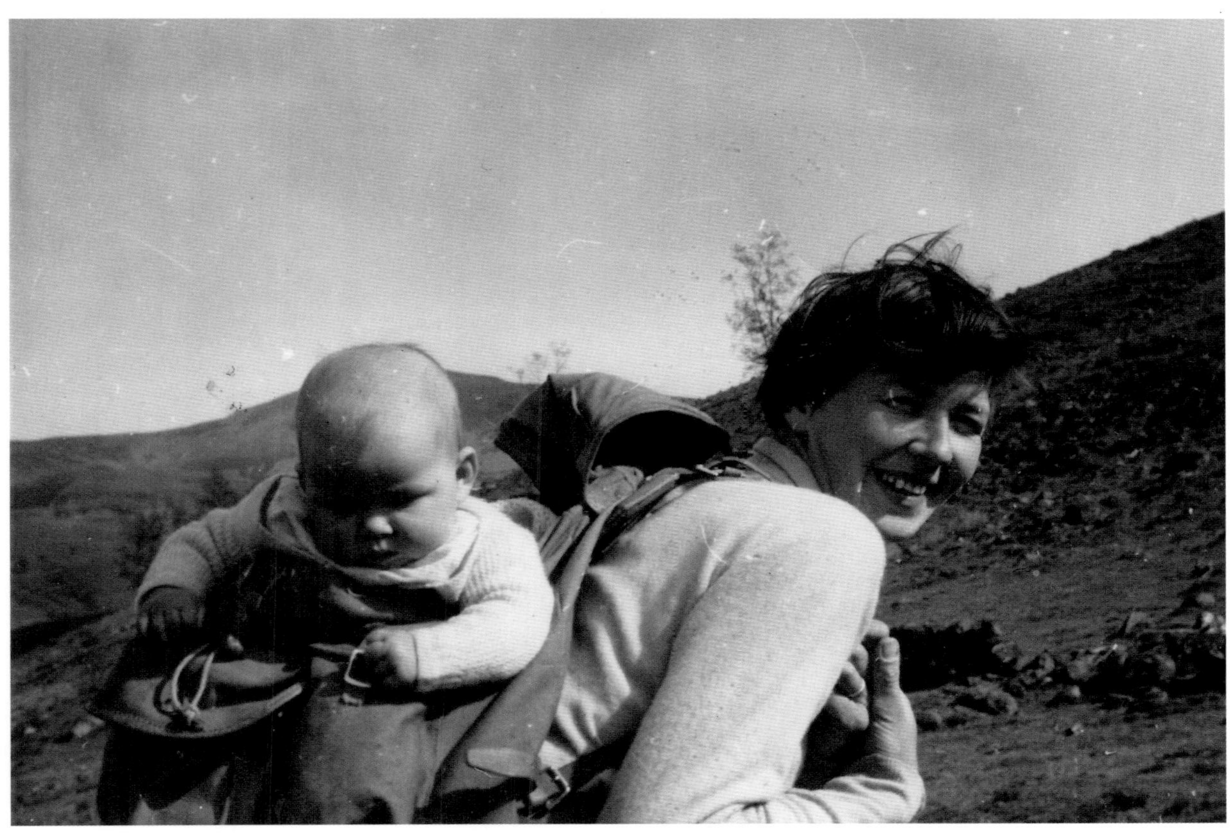

Christian with baby Jenny

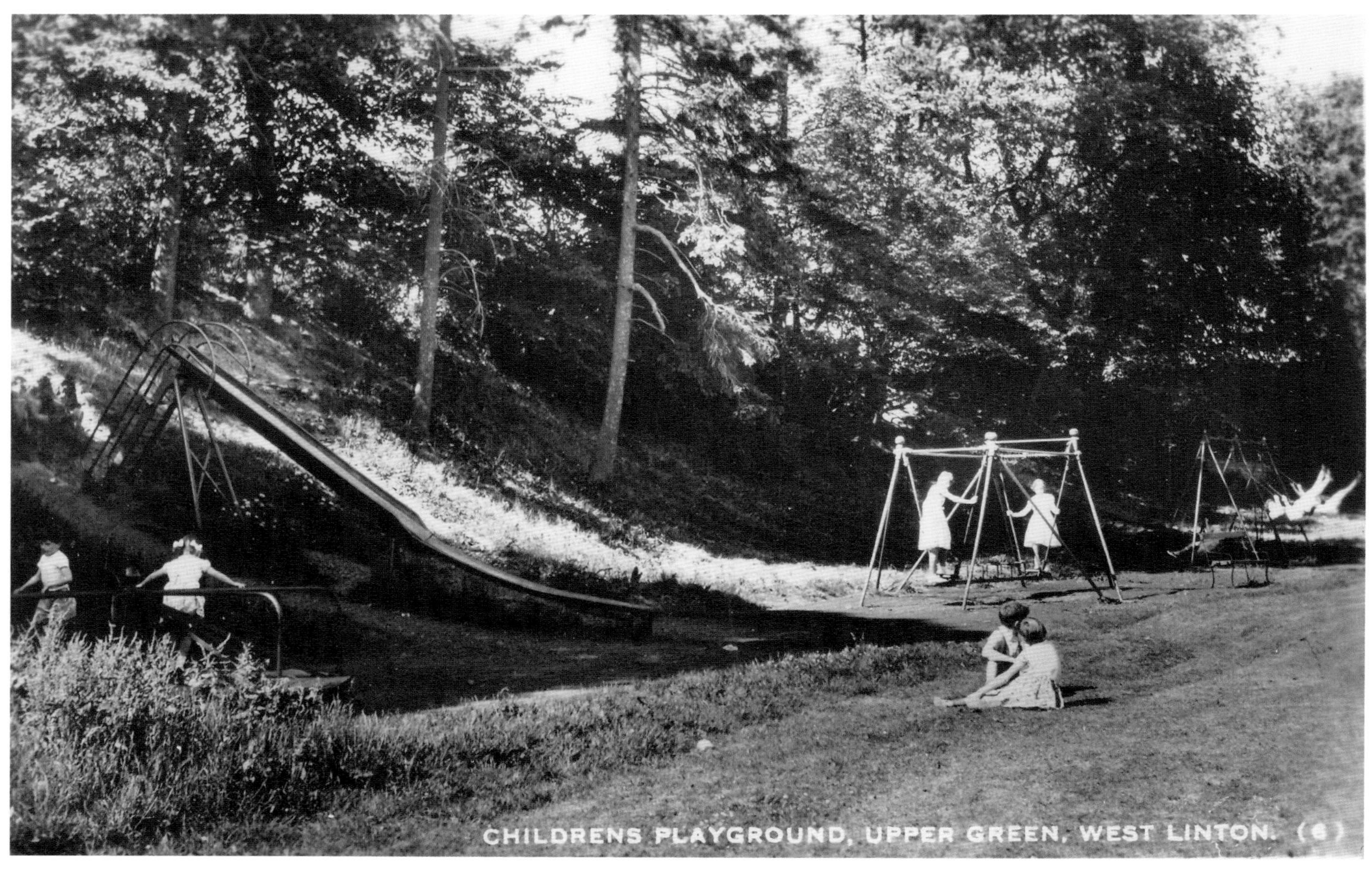

Upper Green swing park, West Linton

her in the loop. Granny was a source of great comfort and warmth to us all, and we owe her thanks for any manners that we ever learned!

For all her awkwardness, and seeming self-absorption, Christian had a deep social conscience. I remember her commitment to volunteering as a teacher in a local literacy course for young people. She worked very effectively with one particular lad who had mild learning difficulties and affectionately called her 'Mum.'

In the '50s and '60s, with hardly any cars, the village was a safe place for children to play. Jenny and I would watch our big brothers racing in their home-made bogies – slats of wood on pram wheels, with a primitive steering system – up and down the Main Street. Along with most people locally, Christian had always used the excellent bus services that ran between West Linton and Edinburgh, seventeen miles away – another era, when you could go to the theatre, cinema, a concert or an evening class in the capital, and get a bus back home. In many ways this was the happiest time of Christian's life, the period when her children were young and dependent upon her, before outside influences, which she feared greatly, could encroach on their lives. She had an anxiety about corrupting forces, perhaps partly because of her father's struggle with addiction, which undoubtedly affected her. This may have contributed to her worries when her first child, Peter, like so many teenagers, rebelled, and asserted his independence. Although their relationship cooled, Peter had much in common with his mother, being a member of the Labour Party and politically active. He graduated in Sociology, and was a lecturer at Stevenson College, Edinburgh. His tragically early death, aged 35, in an appalling explosion, caused by a fractured gas main under the flat in the street where he lived, must have been a doubly devastating blow, since Christian and Peter were never fully reconciled.

***

By this time, Christian and Hugh's marriage had long since broken down, and Yarrow Cottage had been sold. For a few years after the divorce, Christian lived in a small rented cottage on West Linton's Main Street with her youngest son Roger, who was still at school. Roger writes of this period: *I had a definite sense of Mum trying to build her own life beyond family, and she could be very protective of that. Her friendships were HER friendships. An example of this was her renting a little garret at the top of the Royal Mile – her place for Art and escape, I think. I once wanted to use it to crash after a concert (Ian Dury and the Blockheads, no less), and she was very, very difficult to convince, but eventually gave me the key – very cool for me to invite my friends to stay over after the concert.*

I had a bit of the Wagner and Mahler phase, but she also loved Bowie's 'Heroes' and Lou Reed's 'Walk on the Wild Side', as well as some horrendous German jolly mountain songs that haunt me to this day! She had long spells of irritability and fear of loneliness, I think. Also completely random ideas like 'Let's go and cycle in Edinburgh!' OK – two novice riders get off the bus with our bikes and join the traffic. Very crazy, very dangerous and very exhilarating!

***

After her mother's death in 1983, Christian finally settled alone in Chestnut Cottage, where her mother had lived. This would be her last home. Her son David recalls this period as one of change and stability: *Chestnut Cottage, with its lovely garden, offered Mum a sense of security. It also provided Ewan, me and Roger (her three younger sons), with a base, when we were coming and going during summer holidays from university, and preparing to move on to the next stage in our lives. Mum seemed to be able to expand her life there as we moved away. I think some of her best art came from this period. Later, she inherited a stray ginger cat that became pregnant. This was a shock to Mum with her resistance to attachments and dependency, but she persevered, looked after the cat, and kept one of its kittens. My wife Alison and I chose one from the litter; it never lost its aloofness and intolerance of intimacy. When we took Alison's parents to visit Mum for the first time, the ginger cat (still half wild) leaped up the chimney* as soon as we arrived. *Halfway through our cup of tea a black cat burst from the fireplace, across the room and out of the door!*

Christian continued to live, as she'd always done, in Spartan simplicity. Jenny called it indoor camping, and believes that her mother really would have been happiest if time had stopped in the '50s. Jenny recalls: *She loathed change, and as she grew older refused to talk about the past in any way, perhaps fearing the inevitable wash of sorrow that comes with regret.*

I occasionally dropped in on Christian at Chestnut Cottage. I remember one visit in particular. It was some time after Peter's death. Dappled sunlight played on the sitting room window-sill, and a leaf quivered in a breeze outside against the glass pane. Christian said: *I sometimes feel, when I see a leaf like that, moving in the light, that it's Peter - he's there, somehow, communicating to me.* She was very tearful. This was the only time she ever confided in me. For Christian to persist with her art through dark times must have demanded willpower and self-belief. This statement by artist Georgia O'Keeffe comes to mind: *To create one's world in any of the arts takes courage.*

Ewan remembers: *She enjoyed visits from her family and their children. She was never a conventional granny providing homely meals and cups of tea. Instead she wanted to know about the world and what was happening. She had a subscription to The New Statesman magazine and was always keen to discuss the articles.*

Television producer Lucille McLaughlin writes: *The first time I met Christian she was in her garden in West Linton. It was 1993, and I was keen to know what she was like because I had already decided she would be my mother-in-law. Her son Ewan was blissfully clueless of the future I planned for us. I thought Christian would invite me into her cottage where she would sit me down and make me tea in beautiful china cups and feed me cakes just as dainty as the interior of the cottage itself, a bit like Miss Marple's home. For the next quarter century that Christian was in my life she never did make me a cup of tea. She didn't get much chance because on my first visit to the kitchen I offered to put on the kettle. This was only so that I could wash the cups first, as they looked none too clean to me.*

Christian intrigued, inspired and exhausted me in equal measure. She often asked my views on the environment and 'this mad obsession people had nowadays of never sitting still and always wanting to go travelling, flying off at a moment's notice.' The effect it was having on global warming worried her. 'Why can't they just stay at home?' she would ask. 'How can you stand being in one little village, which you rarely leave?' I would think!

She seemed wary of me because I worked in television. On the other hand, she was delighted with me because I lived in Scotland, and so her son was likely to stay in the country if he stayed with me. Roger had emigrated to Australia, shortly after Peter's death. When grandchildren arrived, so too did Christian's knitting…beautiful blankets, hats and jumpers. But of course, she wasn't a typical granny. She treated her grandchildren as equals and loved to play games with them, as long as they were the games Christian wanted to play. She taught them how to plant potatoes and they shared her excitement when it was finally time to dig up the crop. She only stopped gardening aged 89, the year before she died. She

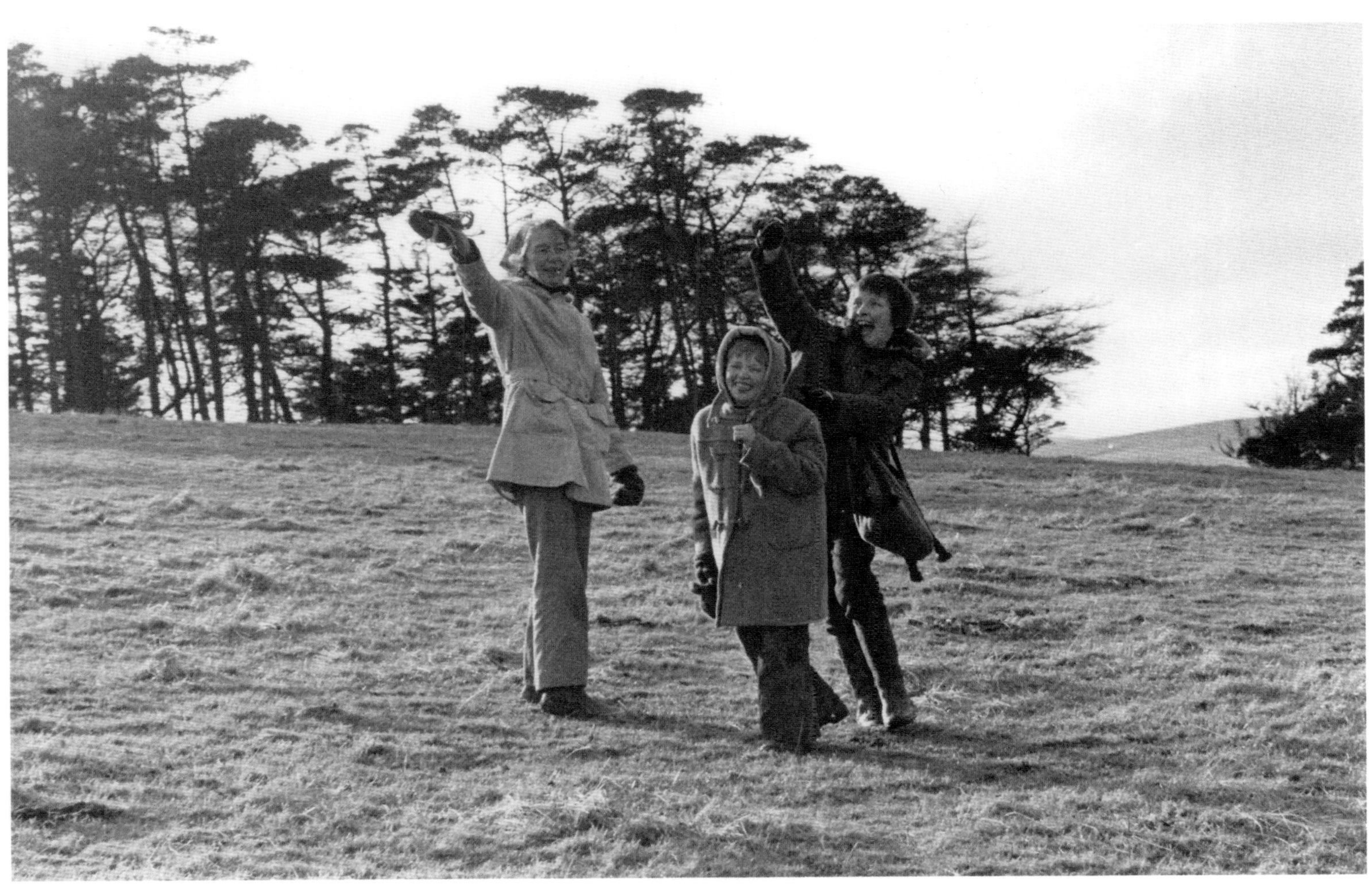

Christian, Roger and David on slopes above the upper Loan

kept her paintings in a large cot in the back room. Now and then we would look through them, and she would take delight in pointing out why she was particularly pleased with the effect she had created of a tree bent out of shape by the wind, or a dead flower with just a suggestion of the orange it had once been. She had great observational skills and she could bring village characters to life in her chat just as she could show such an eye for detail in her drawings and paintings. She appreciated all her grandchildren's artistic endeavours but never gave praise unless she felt it was due.

Christian used to take a bus and two trains to come and visit us on the south side of Glasgow when the children were

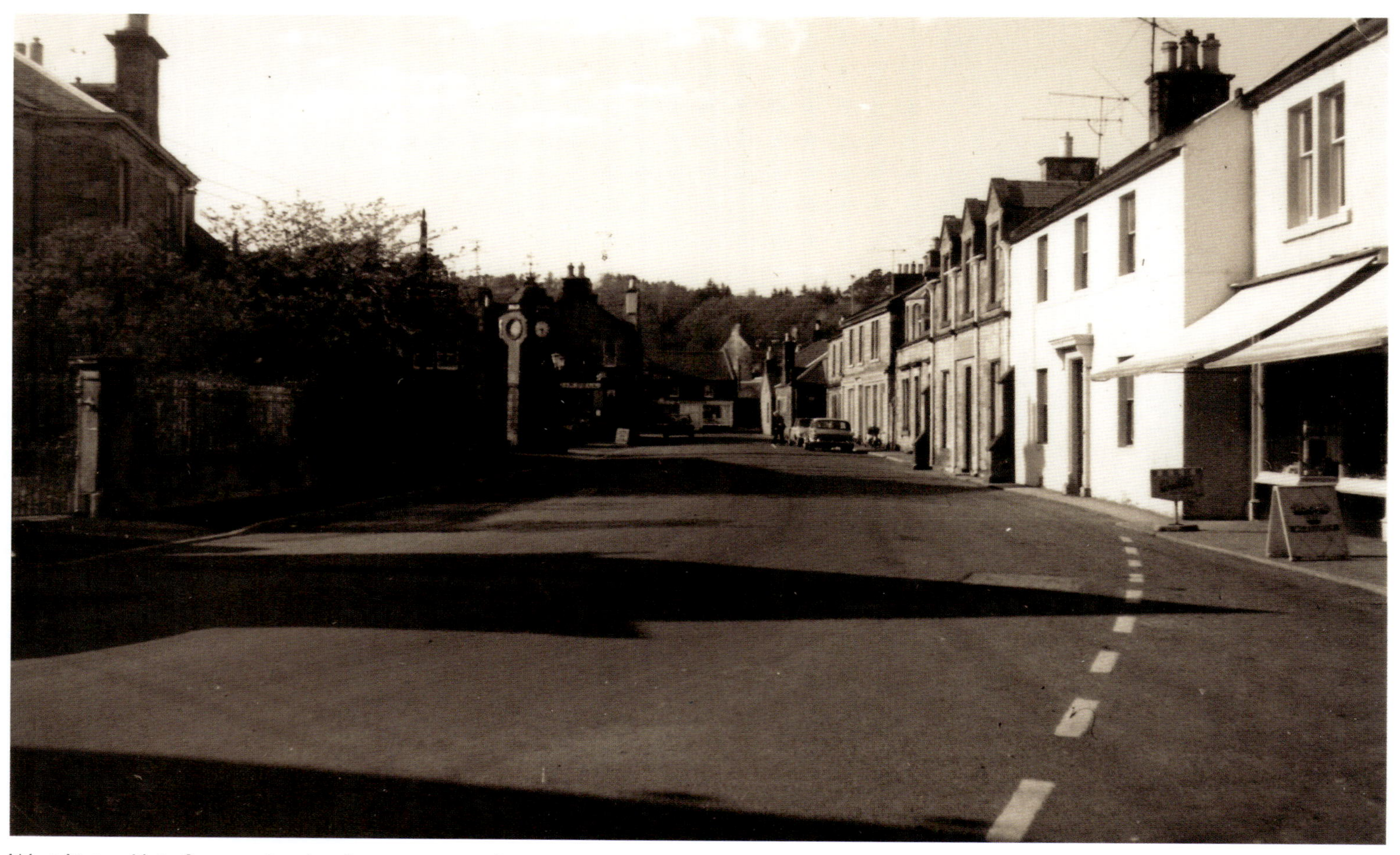

West Linton Main Street, when hardly anyone owned a car

little. At Christmas she sometimes came to stay, on the understanding that it would be for two nights only, we would pick her up, and there would be no alcohol taken by the driver. One year she decided to spend Christmas on her own in West Linton. She was nervous about it, but on balance she decided she liked her West Linton Christmas just fine. And she didn't visit Glasgow again.

As she grew older, she enjoyed swearing. She wanted to know which words the BBC found most offensive. I suggested what they might be, but she wanted them spoken loudly, which I found hard to do. Ewan's cheeks would take on a pinkish hue when she swore. I found it quite charming.

One day when I was with her she decided to let me look in the rear section of the medical cabinet. I was allowed to do *this, she told me, because I no longer worked for the BBC. I was not to make public anything she showed me – photos of a family in idyllic country settings, innocent of what lay ahead of them. Finally, out came Sidney's wartime diaries, pages torn out here and there, written in pencil, long since faded and very difficult to read. She allowed me to take them away on condition that they would never find their way into the hands of the BBC. I had just been thinking that there was a great radio play to be made for the anniversary of Gallipoli, which the diaries might inspire. And that was the only time I saw the contents of the medical cabinet. She was such a contradiction, refusing to talk about the past, but then delighting in a rare look at the photos of people and places of the past, before she shut them out again.*

In her final years, on our visits to West Linton, time would be spent in the garden, Ewan would cook a simple lunch, games would be played – Scrabble, Upwards, Blokus, always accompanied by hoots of delight and exclamations from Christian if anyone beat her. 'Stinker!' 'Mercy!' and those chosen swear words which brought a tinge of pink to the cheeks of her son.

***

Christian had no love for the pressures of the modern world, driven by technology, and the excesses of capitalism. Her friend and neighbour, Virginia Barnes, spent a lot of time in her company during these later years, and writes: *Memories of Christian: sitting in the doorway of her cottage the moment the sun came out, soaking up the warmth. Her laugh, and wringing of hands. Her lively mind. Her diffidence. Christian in her garden, trying to grow veggies, despite a losing battle against Bishop's weed. She was devastated when one of her beloved cherry trees blew down. Her ability to see beauty or interest in the most unlikely of subjects. Cycling with Christian on a hot summer's day up towards Baddingsgill, where we did some painting – magic! Rowing with Christian on the North Esk Reservoir. Her resistance to anything new, ranging from cordless phones to having her chimney relined, to the trees on the way up to the bus stop being pollarded – she was most indignant about this. Banging with a stick on the roof of a car which she considered was being driven through the village too fast!*

And her close friend, the sculptor Susan White-Oakes says: *There was never any small talk with Christian. Subjects for conversation were entered into directly, sometimes across the Main Street in West Linton. 'Susan – what do you think of the election result?' or 'Susan – how can we be going to war with Iraq?' Whatever I had been planning to do at that moment – shopping, sculpture – would be postponed, and we would end up at Chestnut Cottage discussing the subject in question. I never came away from Christian's feeling I had wasted time; whether the subject for discussion had been painting or politics, literature or physics, she was always stimulating company. When my husband and I moved to Tarfhaugh Farmhouse, a mile outside the village, Christian needed a bicycle. There was a selection of old bikes left in our barn, and I managed to assemble a working one out of the parts. This served her for several years until she was given a more up-to-date model. Having a bicycle greatly extended how far she could explore the surrounding countryside, particularly for painting and sketching.*

Down the Bogsbank Road, there were a number of wild raspberry canes and gooseberry bushes, and Christian and I

*would go picking together in the season. She might phone:
'Susan – I will meet you at your entrance track in 15 minutes.
We are going berry picking.' Sometimes I'd drop everything
and go, but sometimes I couldn't. My husband, Christian and
I would go on various cycle rides together. If we returned down
Pirndean, a nearby steep hill, it was a tradition that we would
compete, shouting encouragement to each other, to see who
could reach Tarfhaugh track first by freewheeling all the way.
Three pensioners behaving like ten year olds!*

***

For Christian, West Linton represented a landscape of
nurturing permanence. Her paintings are often (though
by no means exclusively) a luminous encapsulation of a
peaceful idyll, a kind of pure joy in natural beauty and simple
things. I think her creativity was perhaps her solace, a place
in which she was able to shed or channel the agitation she
experienced so often in other parts of her life.

Lucille comments on Christian's work: *I am sure she could
not have painted as she did without the life experience she
had. I can't help thinking that she was drawn to the bleakness
of the landscape around her – to paint trees in winter, bare
and bent by the wind in uncomfortable poses, surrounded by
barbed wire, and strange, deadly crows – rather more than
she was to those glorious floral arrangements outside and
in, canoodling pears on window ledges, and every-day items
around the house.*

I think she was equally drawn to both polarities, just as
she was drawn to Mahler and Lou Reed. It was clear to me,
when I returned to live near West Linton, that Christian's
commitment to art had intensified over the years. Her
work had developed impressively. She'd attended painting
classes locally. John Savory, who signed up for one of these
classes with her, comments: *From day one, it was clear that
Christian's work was on a completely different level from the
rest of us.* She had also studied at Edinburgh College of Art,
where her tutor was Sir Robin Philipson.

She exhibited some of her paintings in West Linton
during her lifetime, but never sold her work in any
organised manner. Interestingly, she did go to the trouble
of having some photographs taken of a few drawings,
and some publicity shots of herself, as if attempting to do
something about promoting her work, but such efforts
were not sustained. In any case, financial transactions were
anathema to her.

Christian is probably beating with a metaphorical stick
at her turf roof in West Linton graveyard, right now,
where she is buried with her mother, in sight of the hills
she roamed, loved, and recorded so beautifully; beating
out her rebellion with that contradictory combination of
self-effacement and voluble assertion, against our efforts
to bring her art, and its context, to a wider public. But she
has left a legacy which cannot be ignored: one woman's
uniquely accomplished expression of a world she loved.

Gerda Stevenson, 2018.

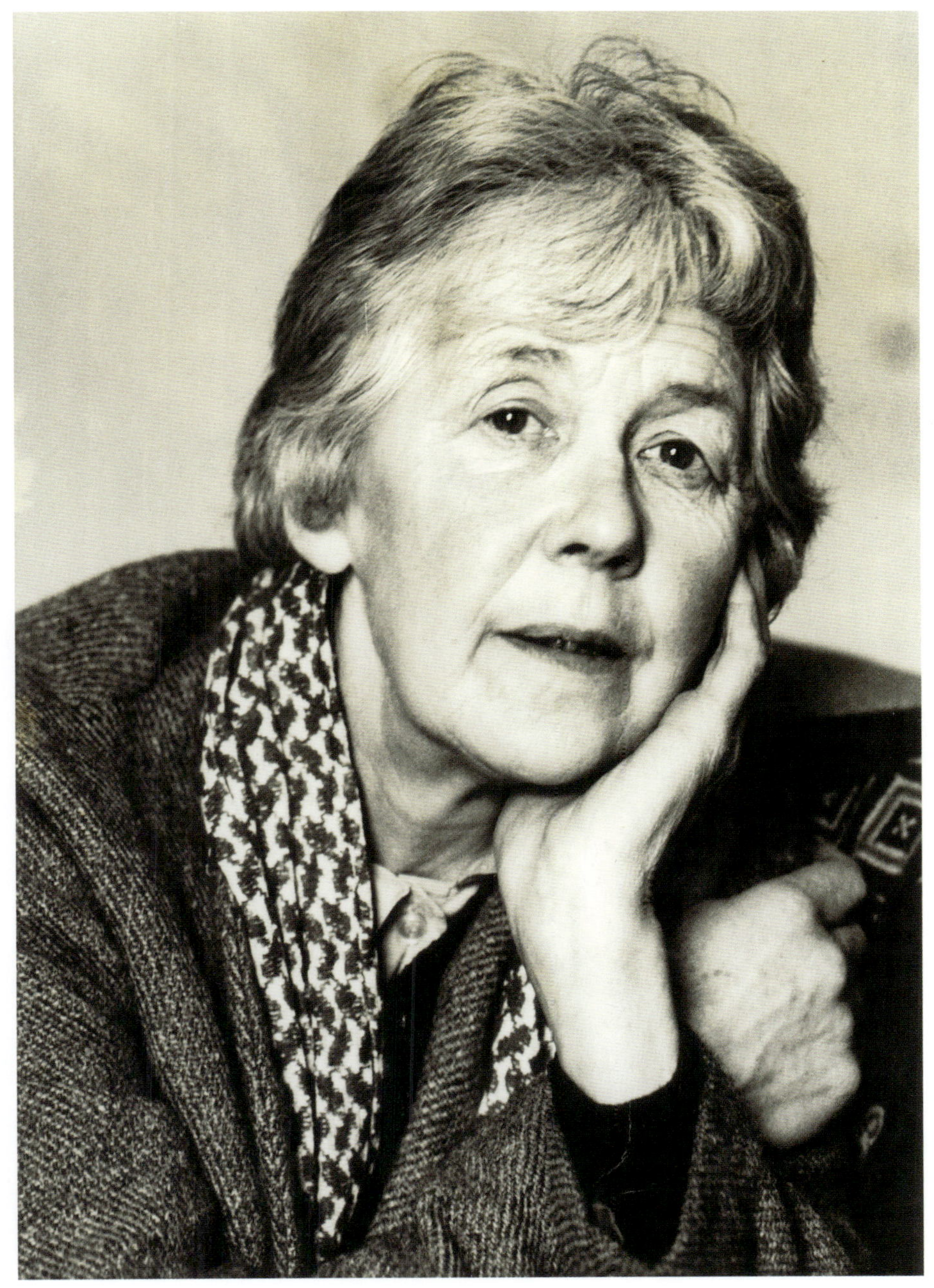

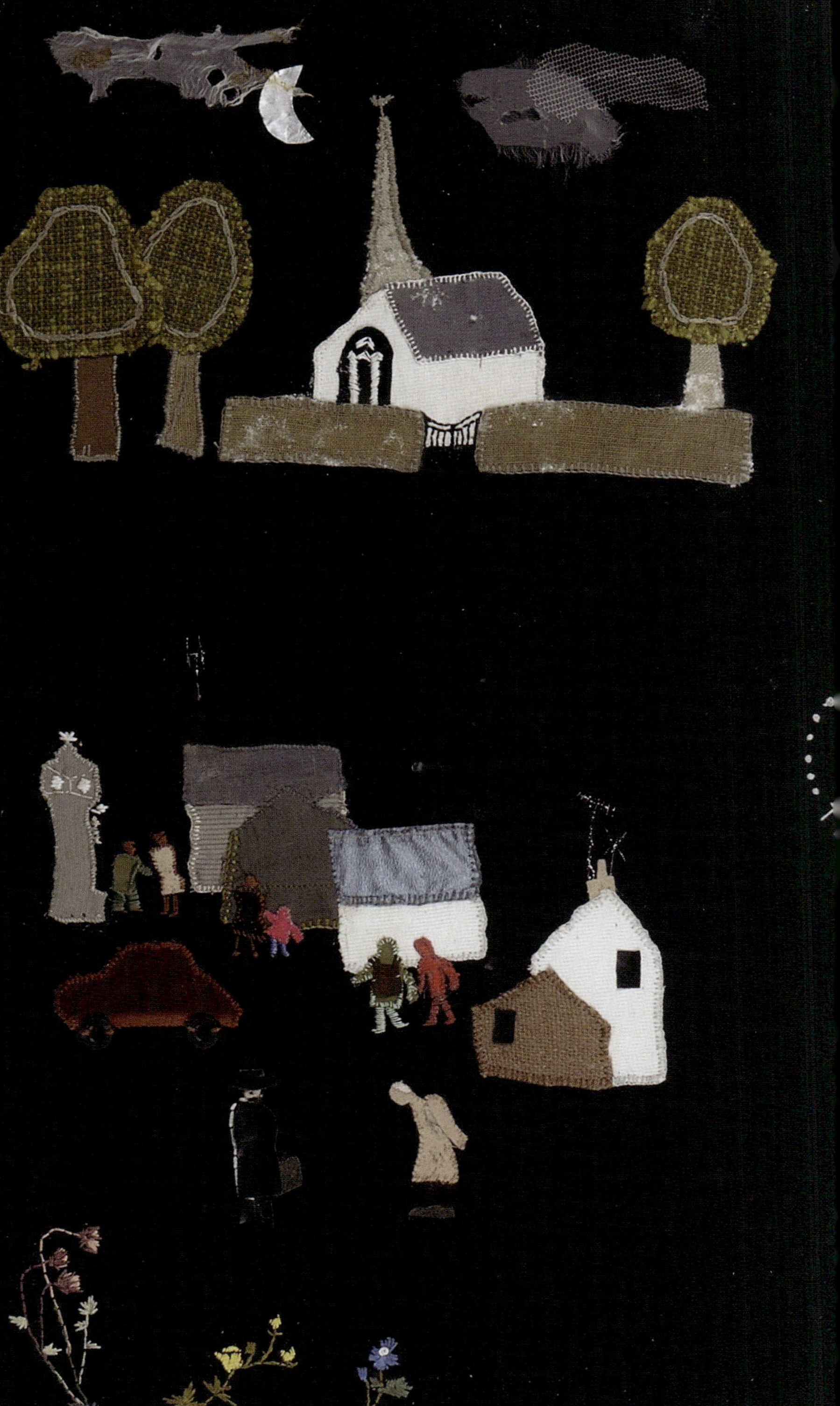

*West Linton: Scraps of cloth bringing
life to the village I love.*

"A wee bag of scrap cloth, needle and thread:
portable and easy to pick up and put down, as
the demands of the day dictate. A tribute to West
Linton: a place I am new to, but will eventually
have called home for over sixty years.
Newly married, I arrive in West Linton. Yarrow
Cottage on the Upper Green: a large garden to
the front, and the back facing onto the green with
the village swing park. From the window, I was
able to watch the children playing there. They had
freedom to roam the village. A perfect place to
raise a family.

Four views:
So here is the Upper Green, with the bridge over
the river Lyne; the swings, and Jim Walter with his
dog Gary going from his house at the top corner
of the green to his garden down by the Lyne. Jim
kept bees and grew vegetables there. His family's
washing is hung out to catch the breeze.
St Andrews church on the Lower Green, whose
lovely spire I would paint many times, when I
moved in later years to Chestnut Cottage.
Life in my garden at Yarrow Cottage: hens and
white fantail pigeons.

fabric applique 597 x 858 mm

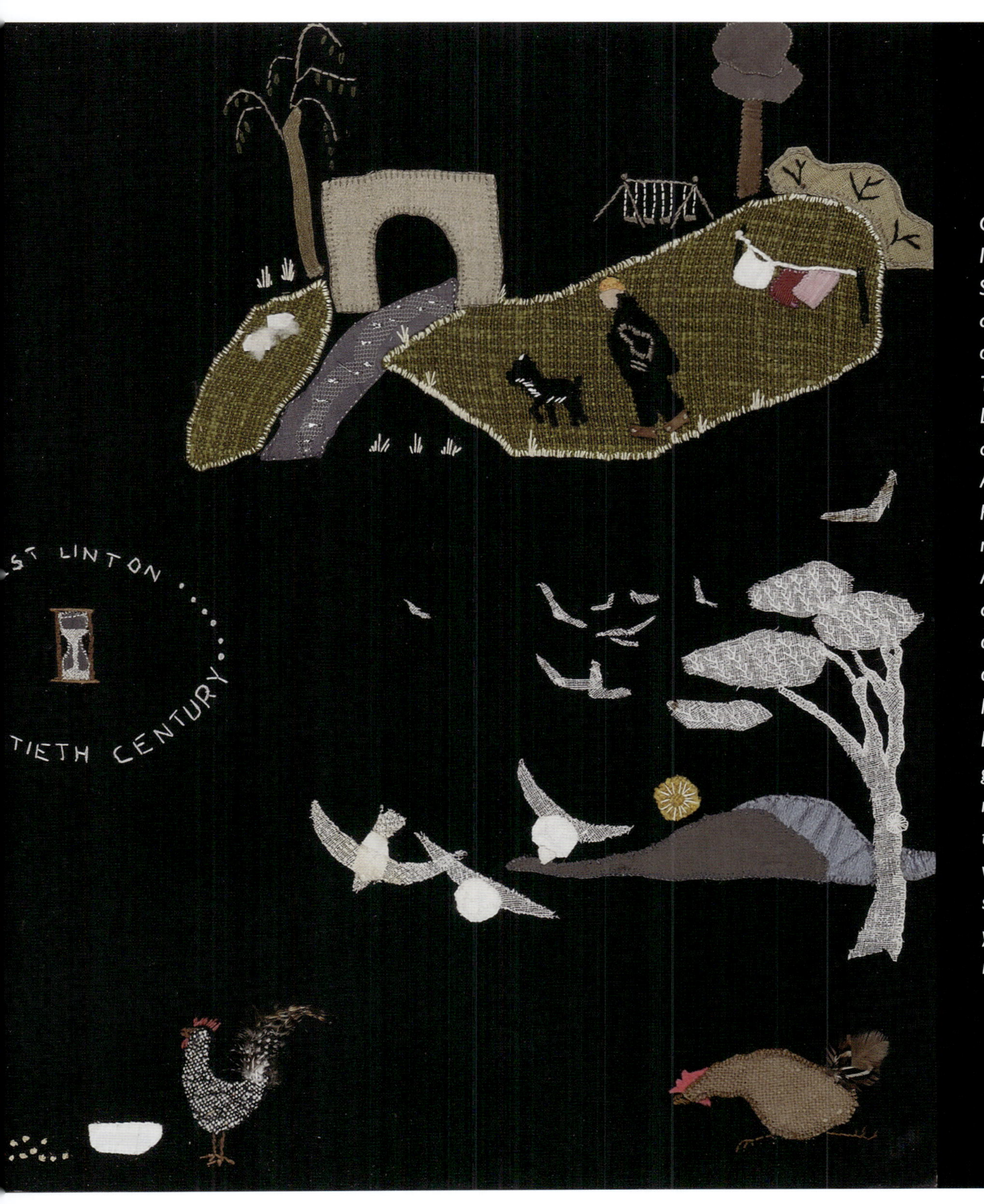

Glancing up the main street, I see the composer Ronald Stevenson in his black coat and hat, and Kenny Paul, bent over – both weel-kent figures. The clock, with its carving of Lady Gifford, watches over the come-and-go of village life. And a memory not pictured here, though always in my mind as part of the scene: the A702 was widened in the 60s, causing traffic to go faster, and one winter, a lorry, carrying oranges, skidded on ice, sliding half-way down the wooded bank above the swings. Its golden load tumbled over the road, and all the way down to the play park. Villagers hurried with bags to be filled. Houses smelling of oranges! A few years later, the swing park was moved to the Lower Green."

"These are the places I have wandered and loved –
safe places close to home. Places I can reach with a baby
in the pram and toddler perched on top. Not too far for the
other three, or for the old dog. I lay down a store of visual
memories. I will return.
A south facing sunny bank, sand for little fingers to dig in,
jam jars filled from the shallow burn to make miniature
rivers, waterfalls and dams. Cool water for hot feet, a
bent pin crudely tied to thread, and attached to a garden
bamboo cane – ever optimistic that a wee minnow will be
inveigled to leave the safety of the overhanging bank and
the deeper reaches of peaty brown. The bank of the Lyne
is perfect, not where the day-trippers spill onto the Green,
but further upstream, opposite the Pantiles where we will
be alone to rest and play.
The arch of beech trees that shade the Golf Course Road
in summer; almost immediately we can leave the road and
find ourselves under that glorious canopy where the children
play in the rotten trunk of a fallen giant. They paddle to
other worlds and so we make it our own Canoe Wood. A
delight for me too as sweet wild raspberries abound and
jam brings back summer memories in the cold winter.
Left past the golf course and left again onto the old Roman
road towards Slipperfield – this place, we called the Mousey
Holes. Were there mice or just little tunnels in a sandy
bank? The heat of the sun and the view south to Broughton
Heights; ruins on either side of the track. Nettles deter the
children who long to climb on the old worn stones. Nettles
are signs of human habitation. I feel this everywhere: a land
well used, harsh in reality – marginal."

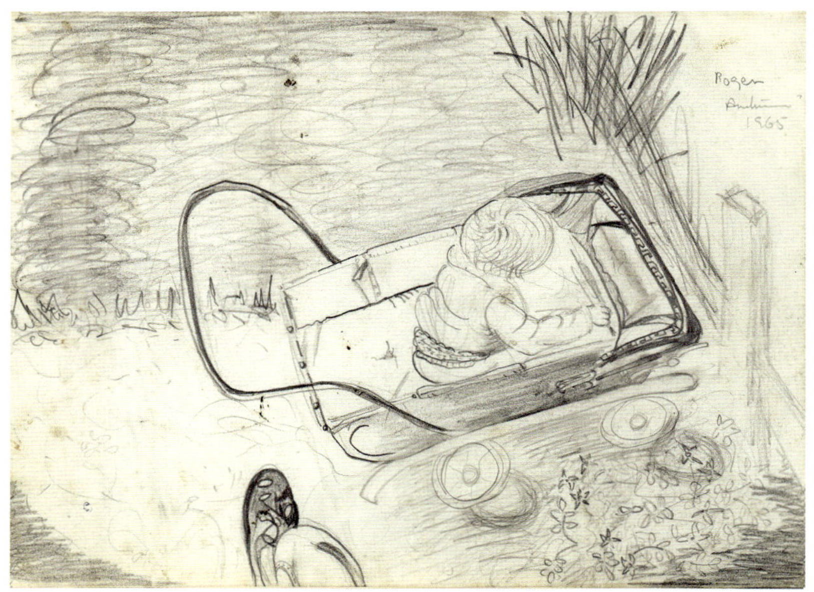

pencil 250 x 350mm

(opposite) ink, watercolour 760 x 470mm

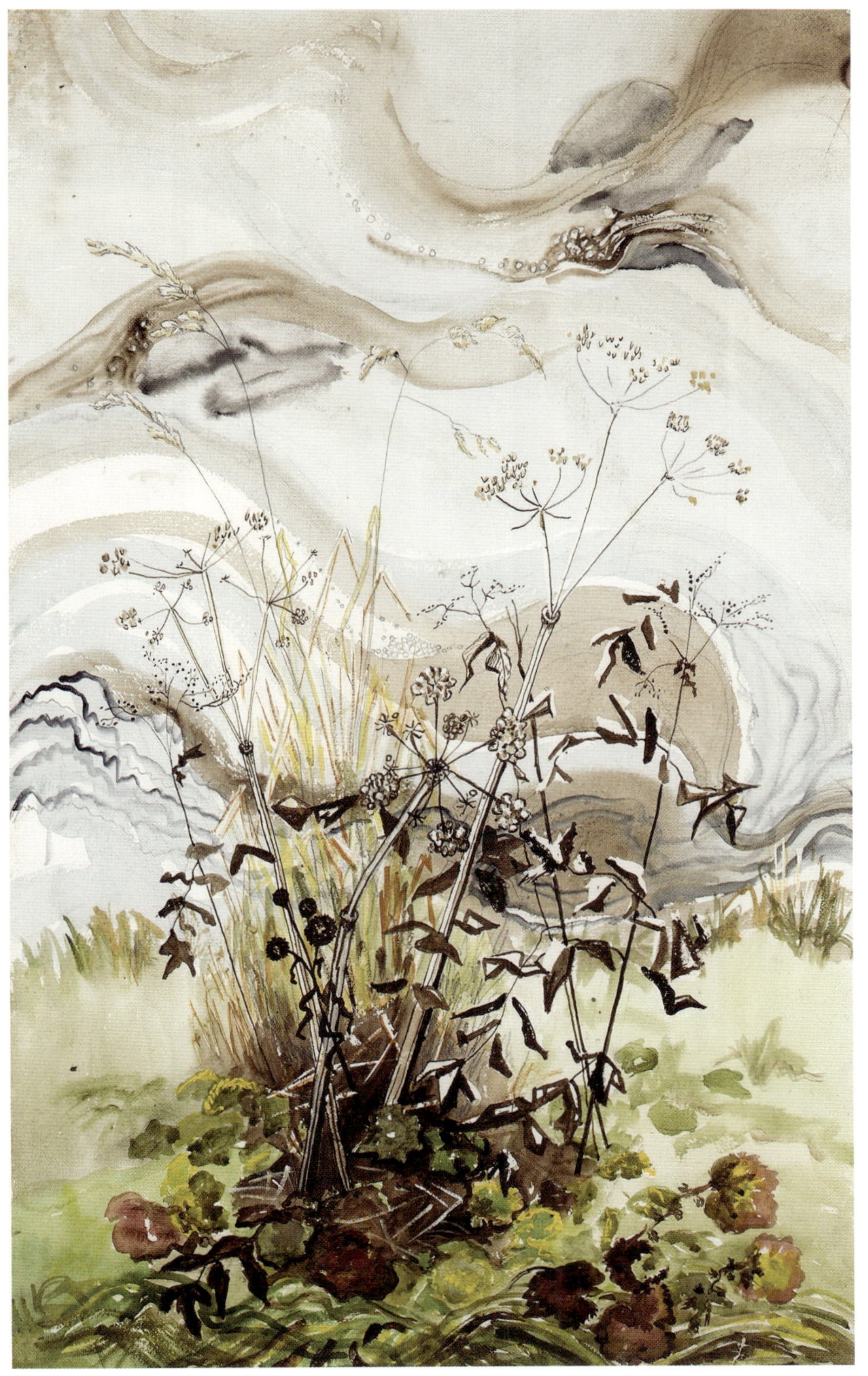

"Lynedale – a secluded place of genteel splendour, with its stately home sloping down to the river. Before we get there the boys clamber up into the woods on the left, and here we spend the afternoon in the Island of Monsters. When older and bolder we are able to go further upstream on a high bank and meet a tributary that falls to join the Lyne in a tumble of water, aptly named Crooked Jock. Old stone remains of a mill – lint perhaps? Another day – children must be older as the track is rougher – we find our way to the top of the Loan where the Pentlands open to the east, Mendick sits in comfort to the west, and the slope lining the Loan is topped with Scots pines, with their limbs akimbo. Did the farmer or the laird know the pleasure they would give to the eye decades ahead of planting, or were they just a boundary, a windbreak? Looking across to Stonypath: a pond up here, from which ancient mare's-tails protrude from the peaty water. More ancient things are yet to be found in the Siller Holes. South of the village, out along Bogsbank Road to the bridge over the Lyne: another river bank, spindly willow and birch. Upstream – a confluence, but thistles bar our way and spiky leaves hugging the ground make the children cry. Another time we'll explore and revisit the rough ground with the heady scent of gorse in bloom. I see the beeches on the slopes up towards Castle Law. I'll be back."

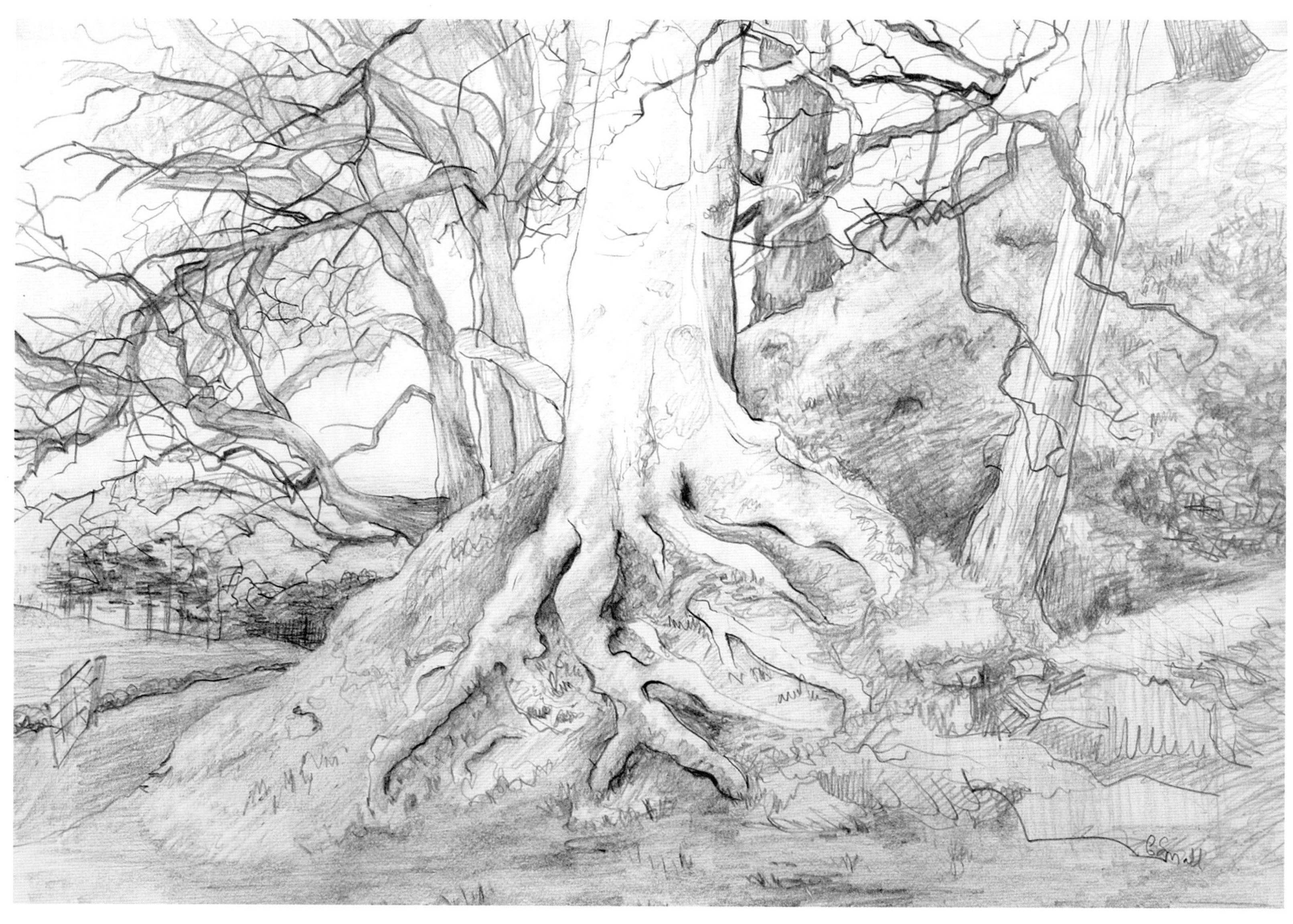

pencil and watercolour 285 x 407mm

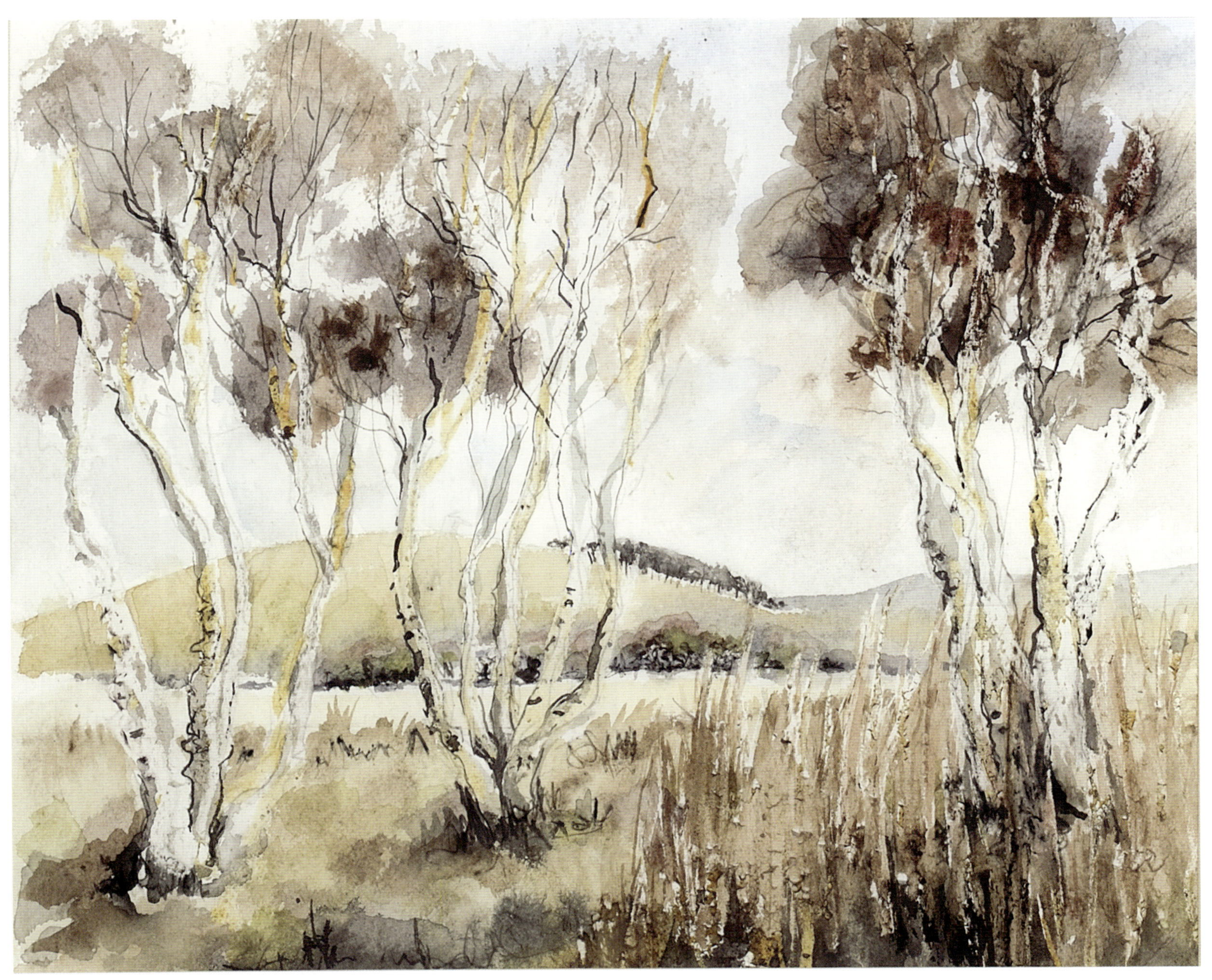

watercolour, ink 267 x 337mm

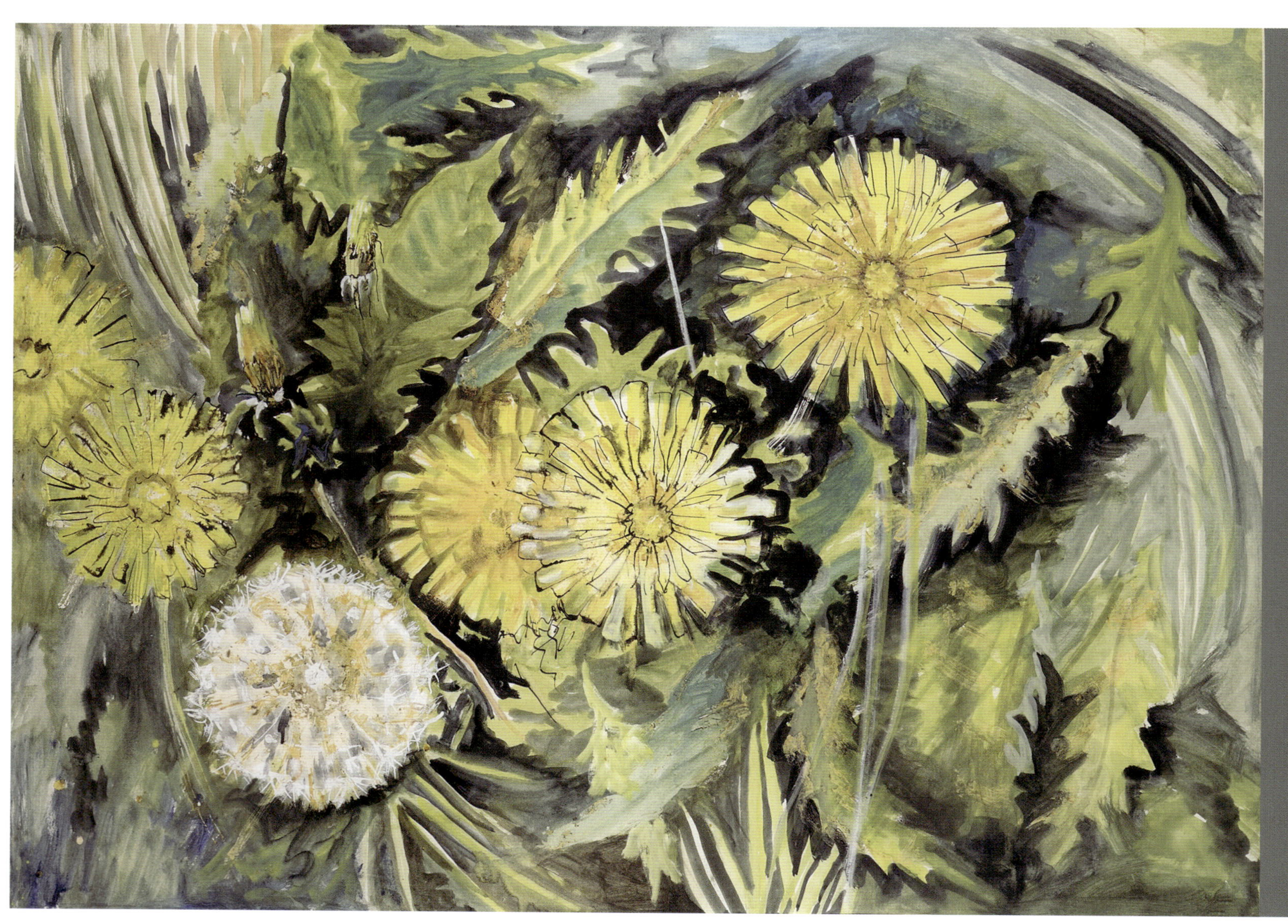

watercolour 510 x 720mm

Dandelions

You clamour at my retina, a cascade
of cartwheels, demanding paint
from my palette, five noisy suns
bursting from earth, like children let out
when the school bell rings;

your lion-teeth leaves scythe green rhythm
all around each brazen face, a dance so bold
even the old among you, that single downy head,
seems eager to play a part – its hair might shake loose
any moment, and poised buds could flare
into flower before I know it. I swear I can smell
the fierce tang of bitter milk coursing through your stalks.
My pen and brush dash across paper, splash, sweep
and thrust, to catch your untamed life – anything but still.

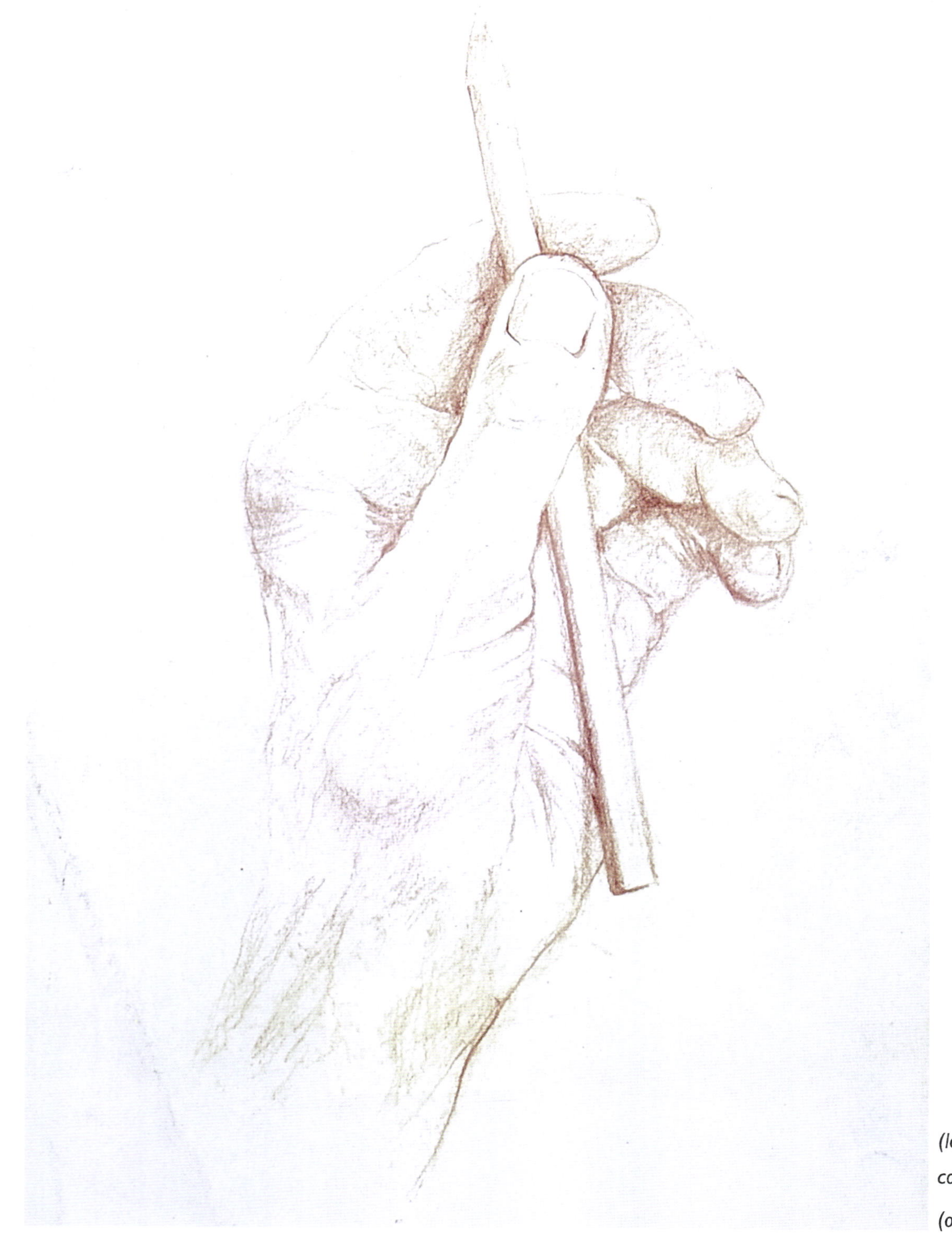

(left)
coloured pencil 300 x 210mm

(opposite) pencil 400 x 286mm

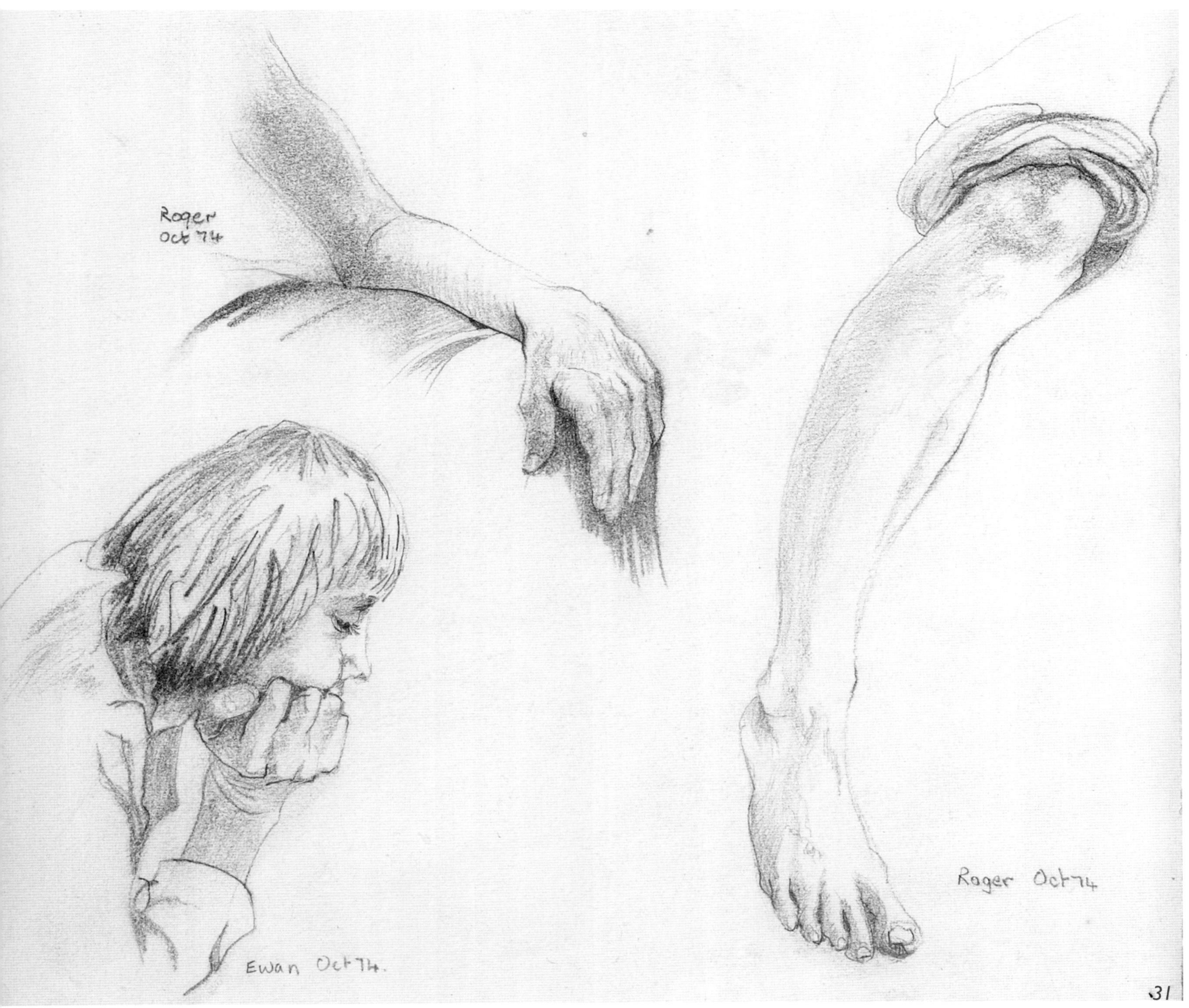

31

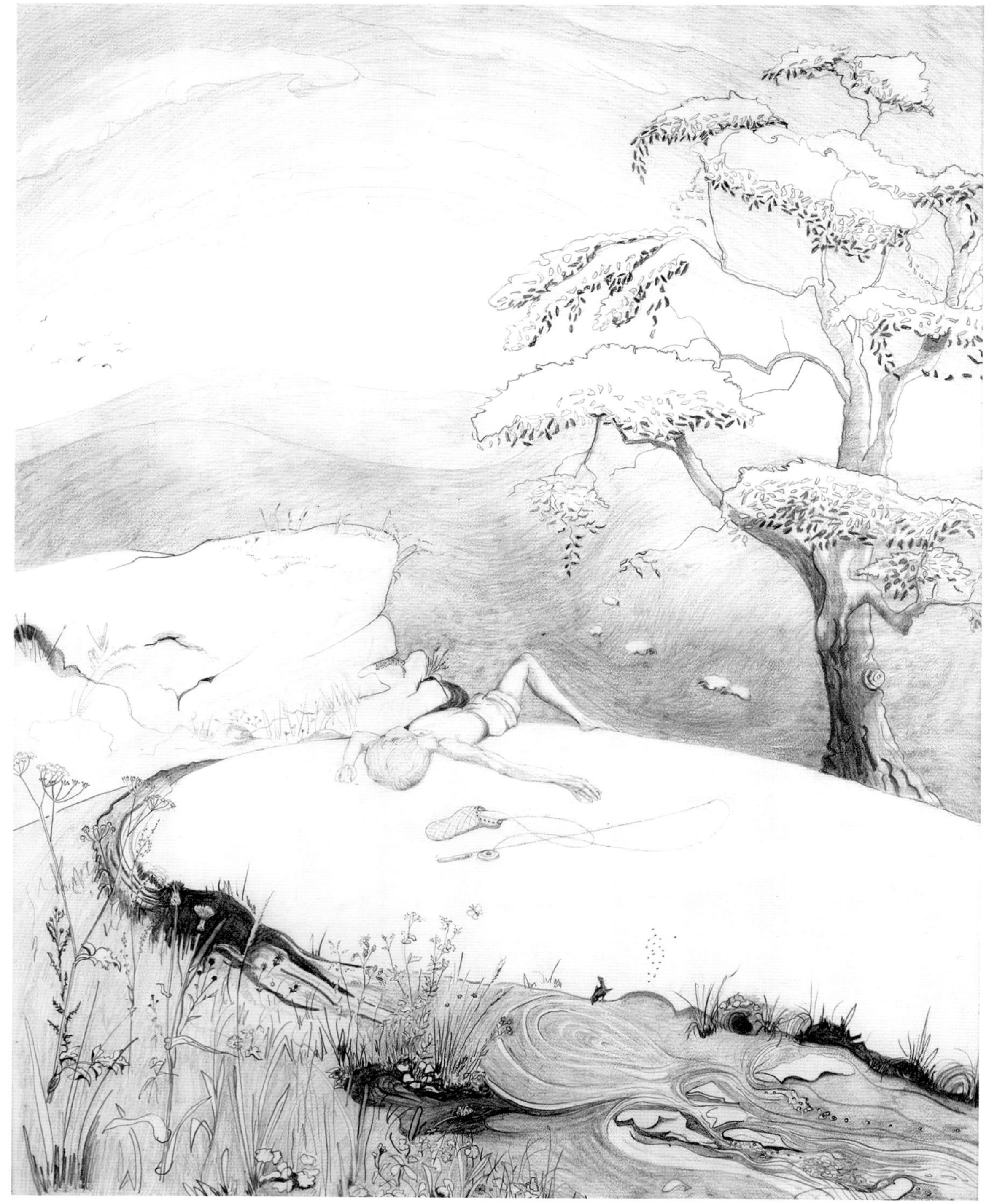

"A dream: a gentle burn meanders, bubbling over the peaty stones. A single Scots pine, a rocky outcrop, sheep and birds in the distance. I can smell the warmth, and hear the water and the crackle of plants as they dry and expand in the sun. Roger, my youngest, at the centre. No wiry young boy would stay on the prickly grass when he could be fishing, paddling or jumping off that rock; did he really lie there as I drew him? I forget now, but the image rests on my mind as quiet perfection – an idyll composed of the many parts that make my love of this rough border country so deep; and a realisation that my exploration is tied up in motherhood."

pencil 622 x 510mm

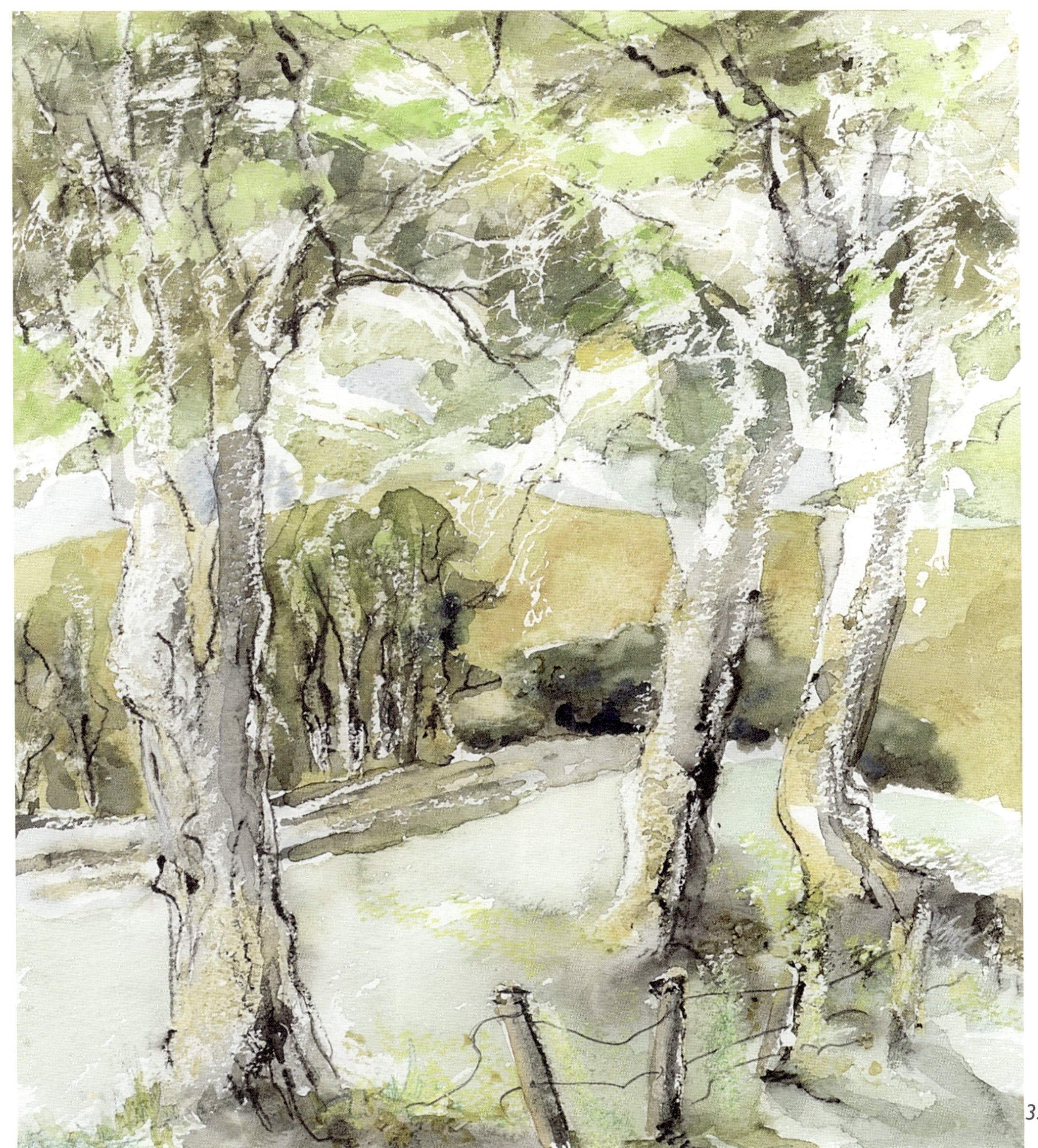

watercolour and ink
320 x 280mm

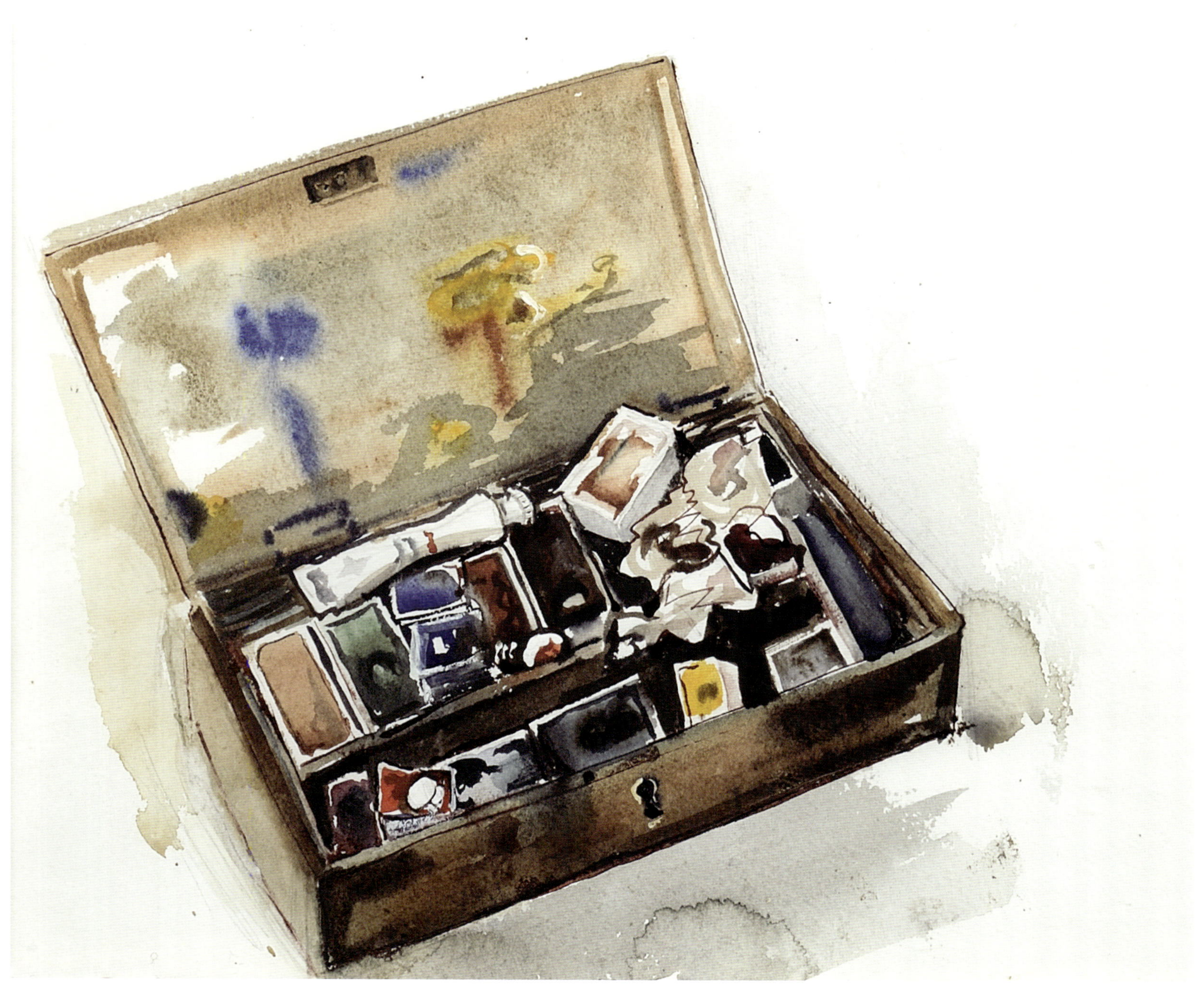

watercolour 275 x 360mm

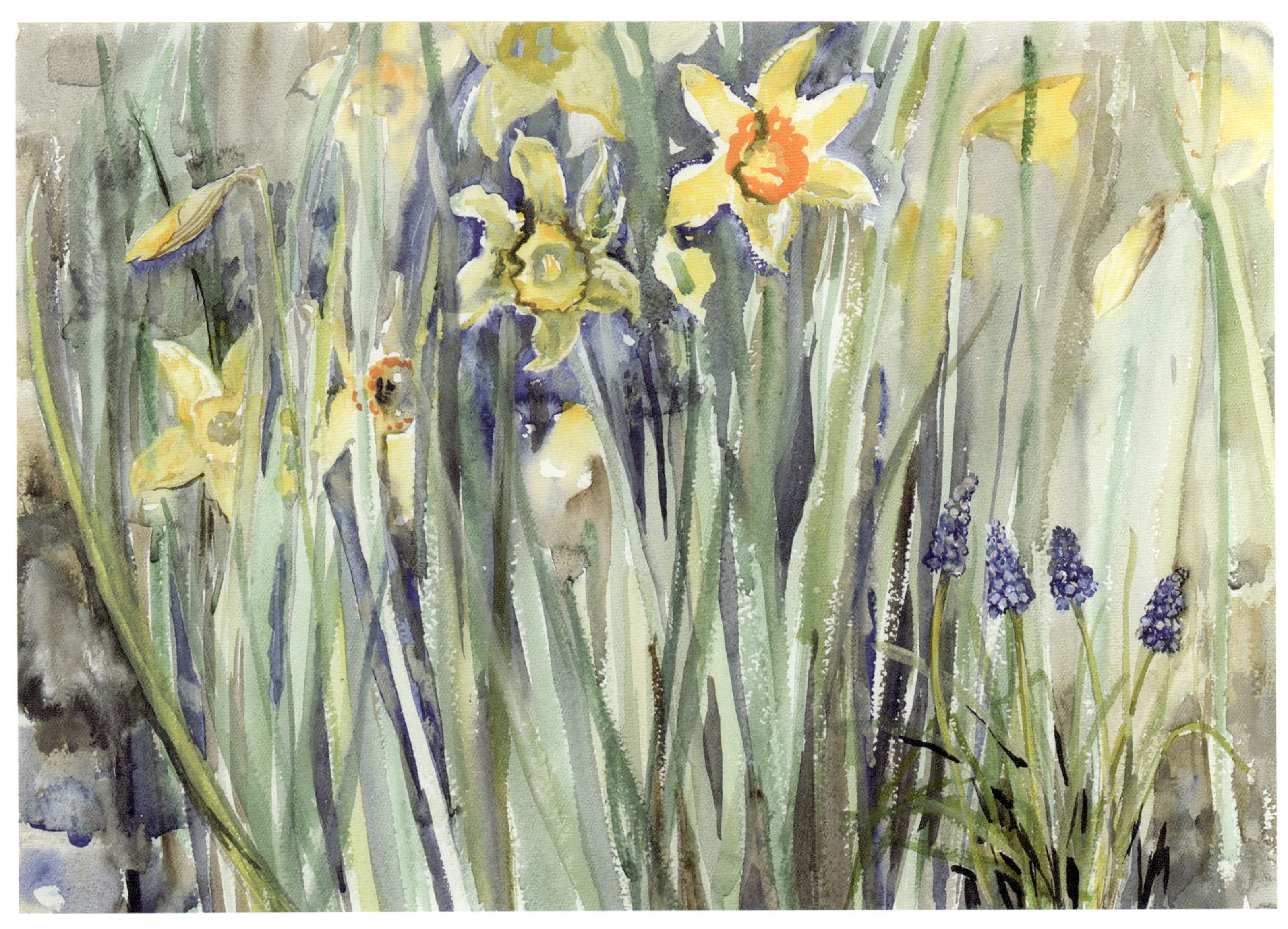

watercolour 381 x 540mm

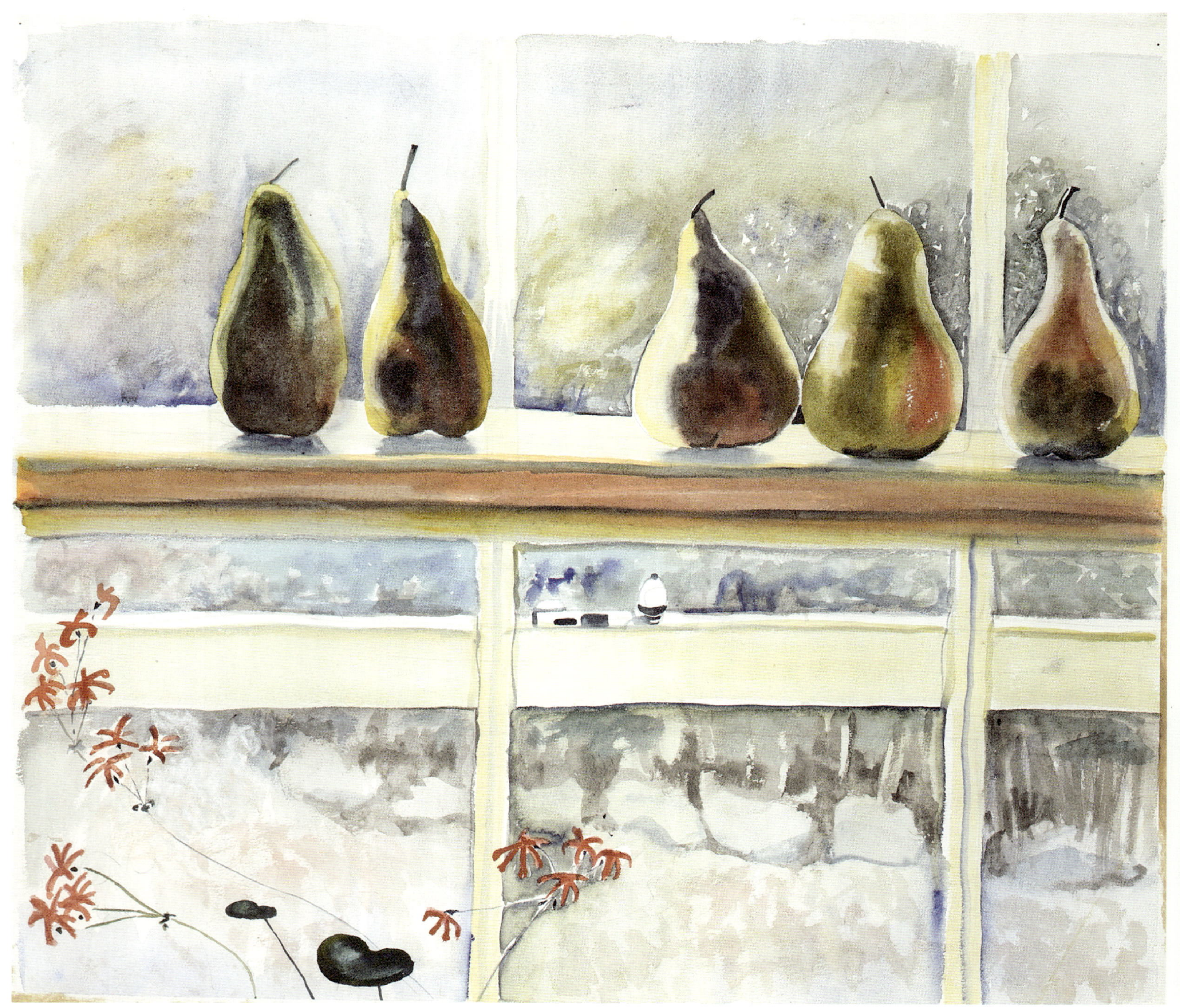

Conference of Pears

They gather in the window frame,
five ladies, conferring on the ripeness
of their fecund bellies; snow throws light
on the slight incline of their necks, as one leans
into another, with the murmur of female sharing,
stalks like tongues, comparing notes –
whose skin is tight as a drum, whose
is softening, who will be the first to deliver
sweet flesh in such unseasonal weather?

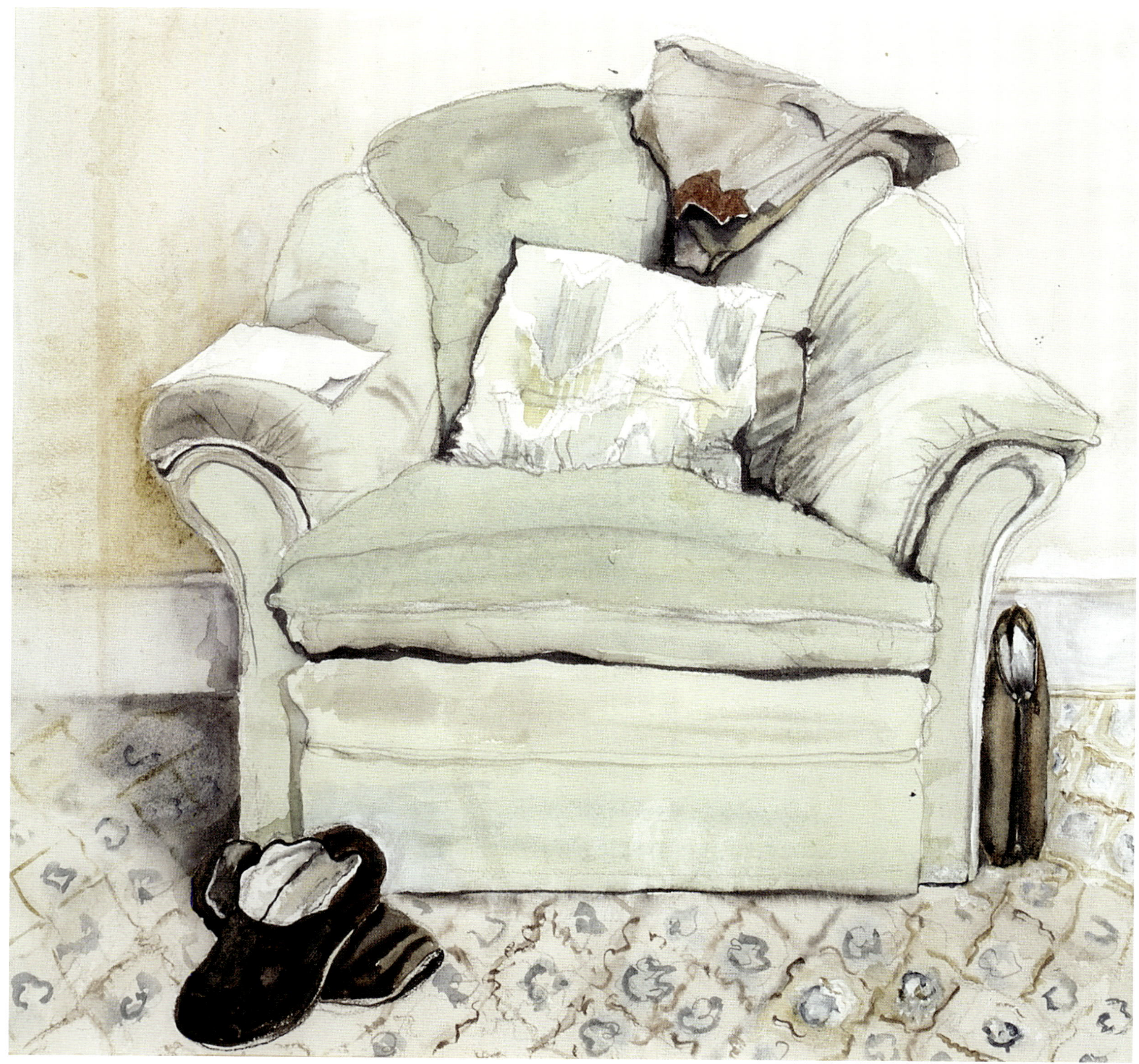

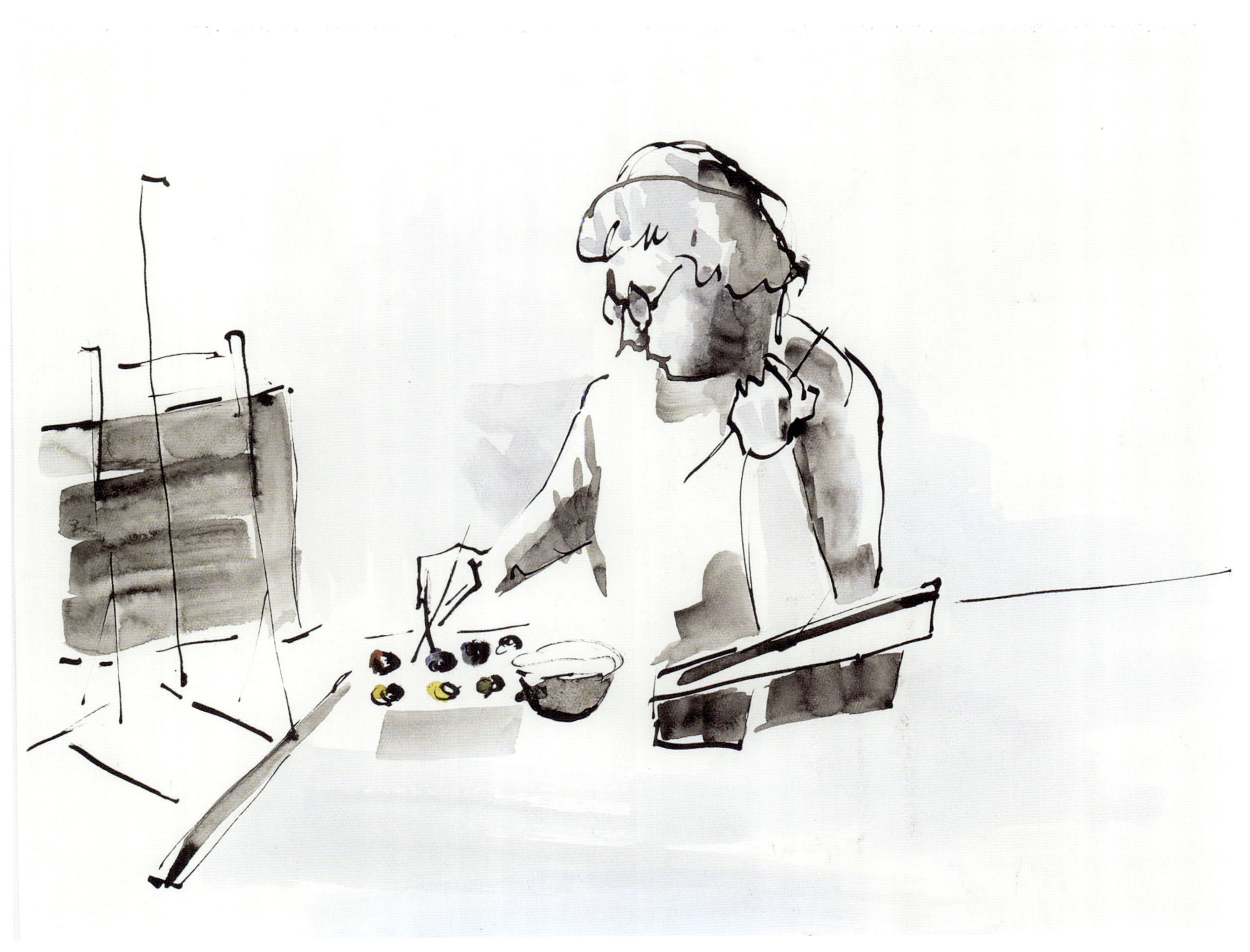

(above) ink and watercolour 330 x 290mm

(opposite) watercolour 335 x 305mm

Tulips

Only yesterday, it seems, red-cupped blooms
pulsed their colour through the room
in summer heat; I marked the moment,
though not on paper, and now, too late,
parched stalks droop their spectral freight,
leaves darken; a stamen mourns
its naked fate to a fading neighbour,
life-blood drained from the scene;

time to rethink - let line predominate:
I'll give blue arteries to inanimate things
(drapes and table cloth), and stroke my brush
down the jug's full belly, from lip to base
in one black sweep, to quicken all.

chalk, ink and watercolour 373 x 290mm

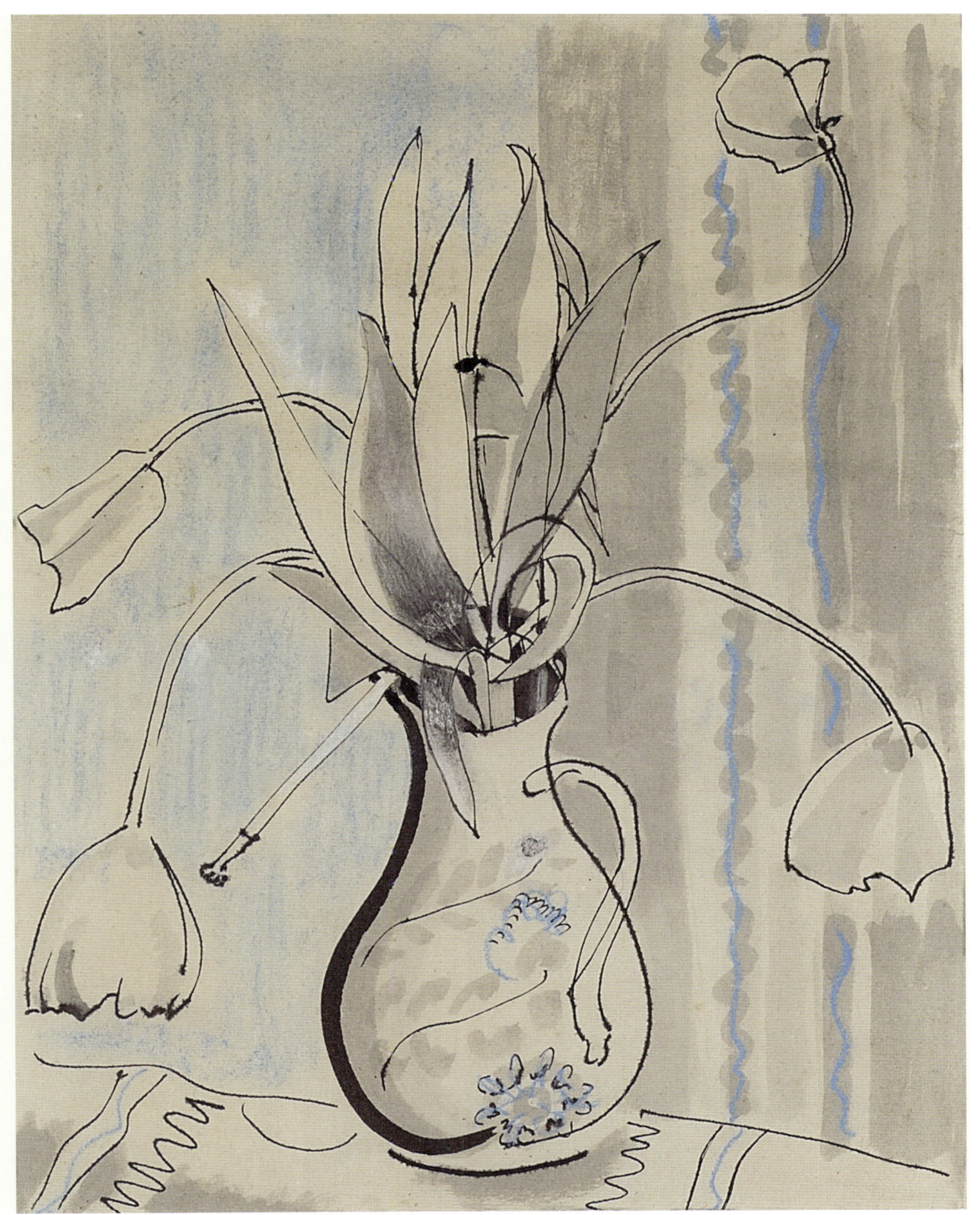

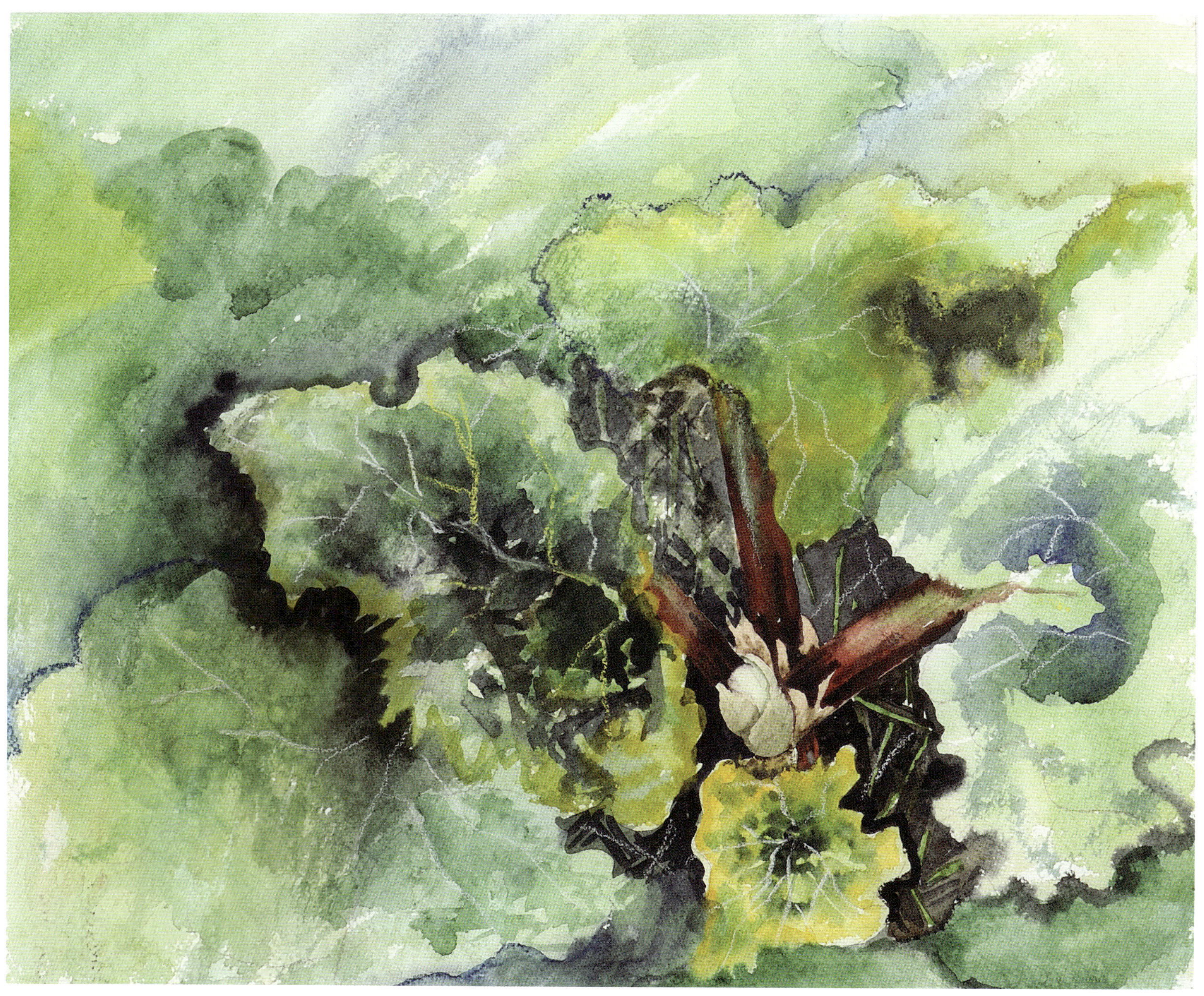

watercolour and chalk 362 x 441mm

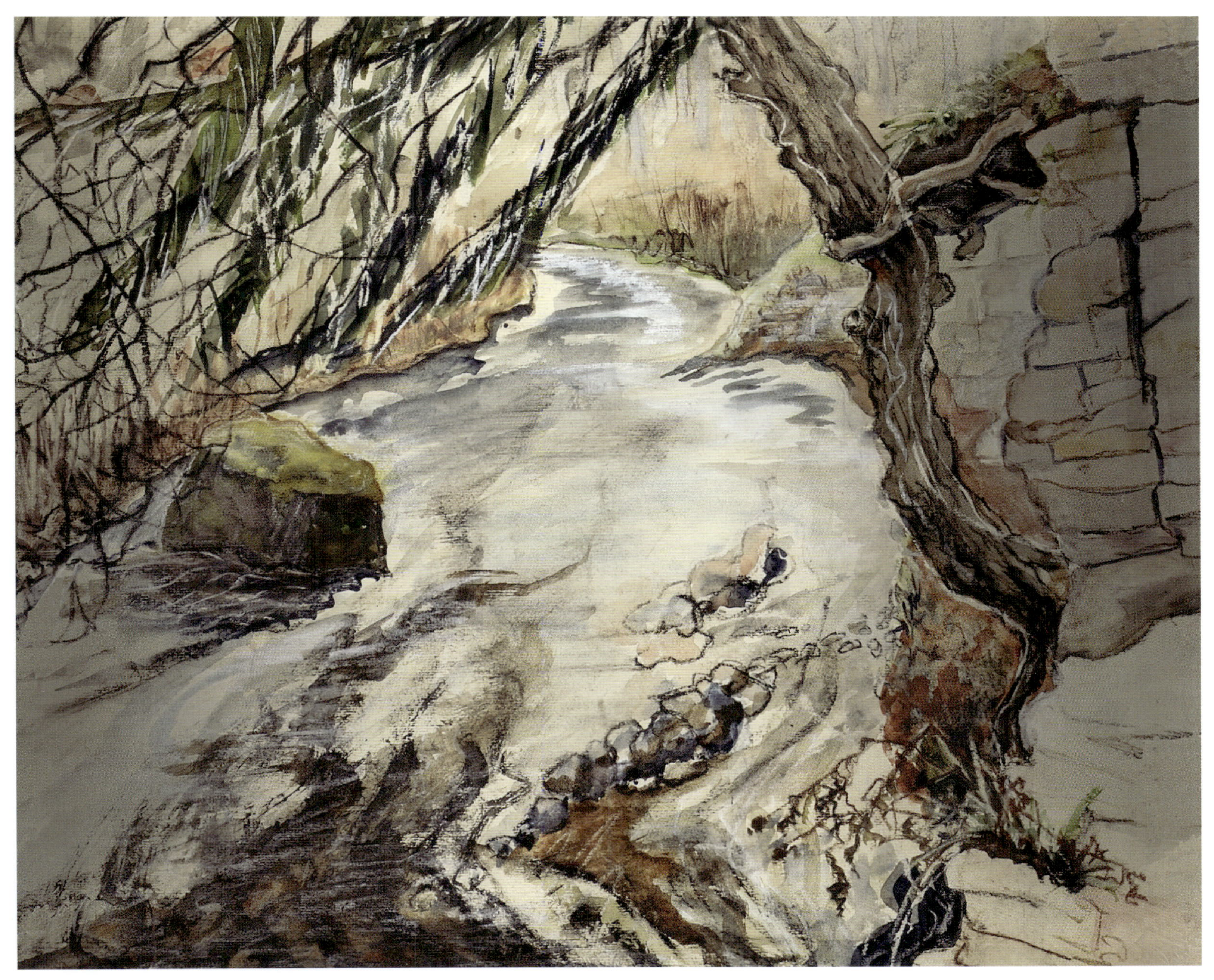

watercolour and chalk 370 x 460mm

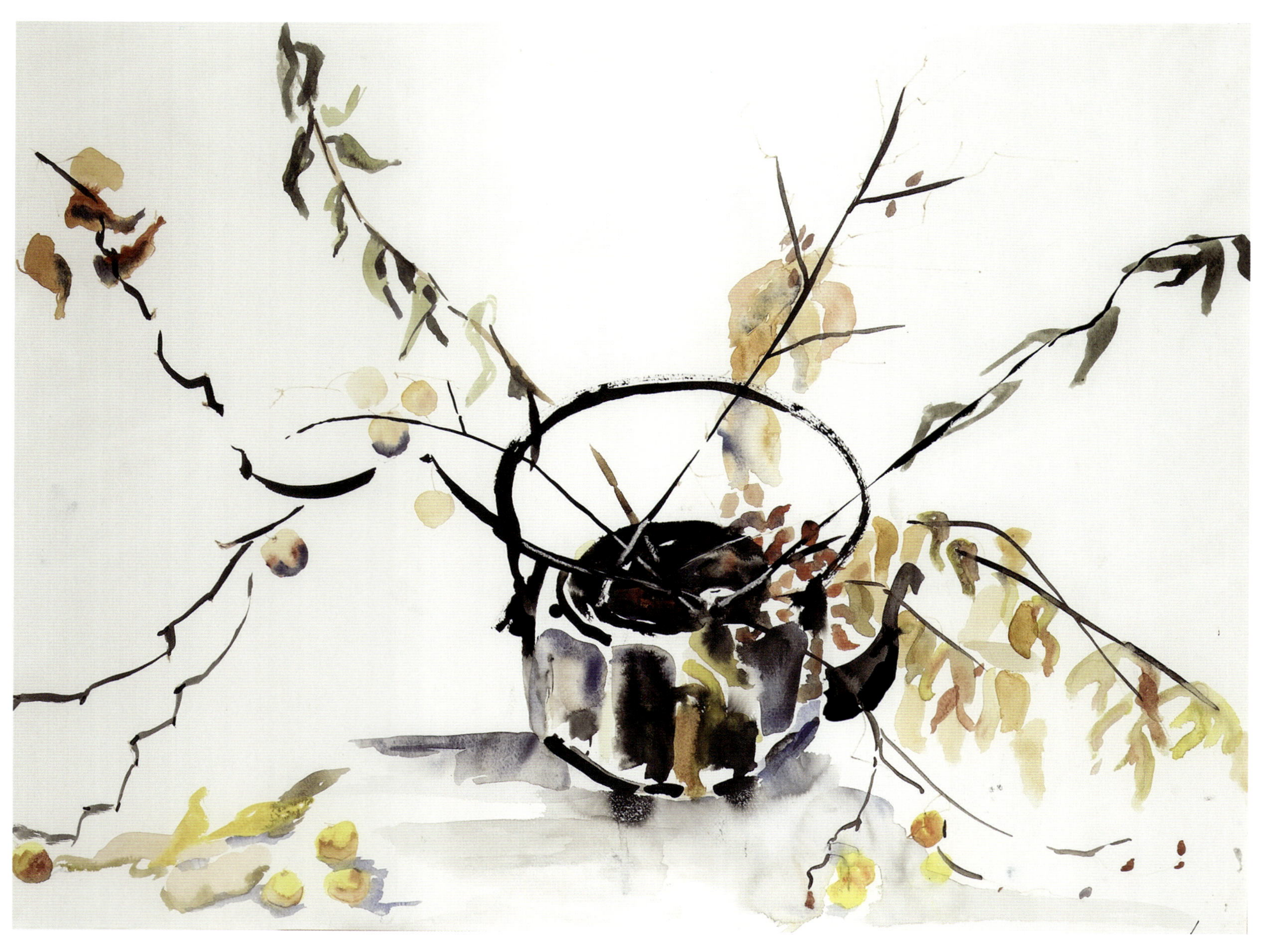

(above) watercolour   485 x 666mm

(opposite) watercolour and ink 310 x 345mm

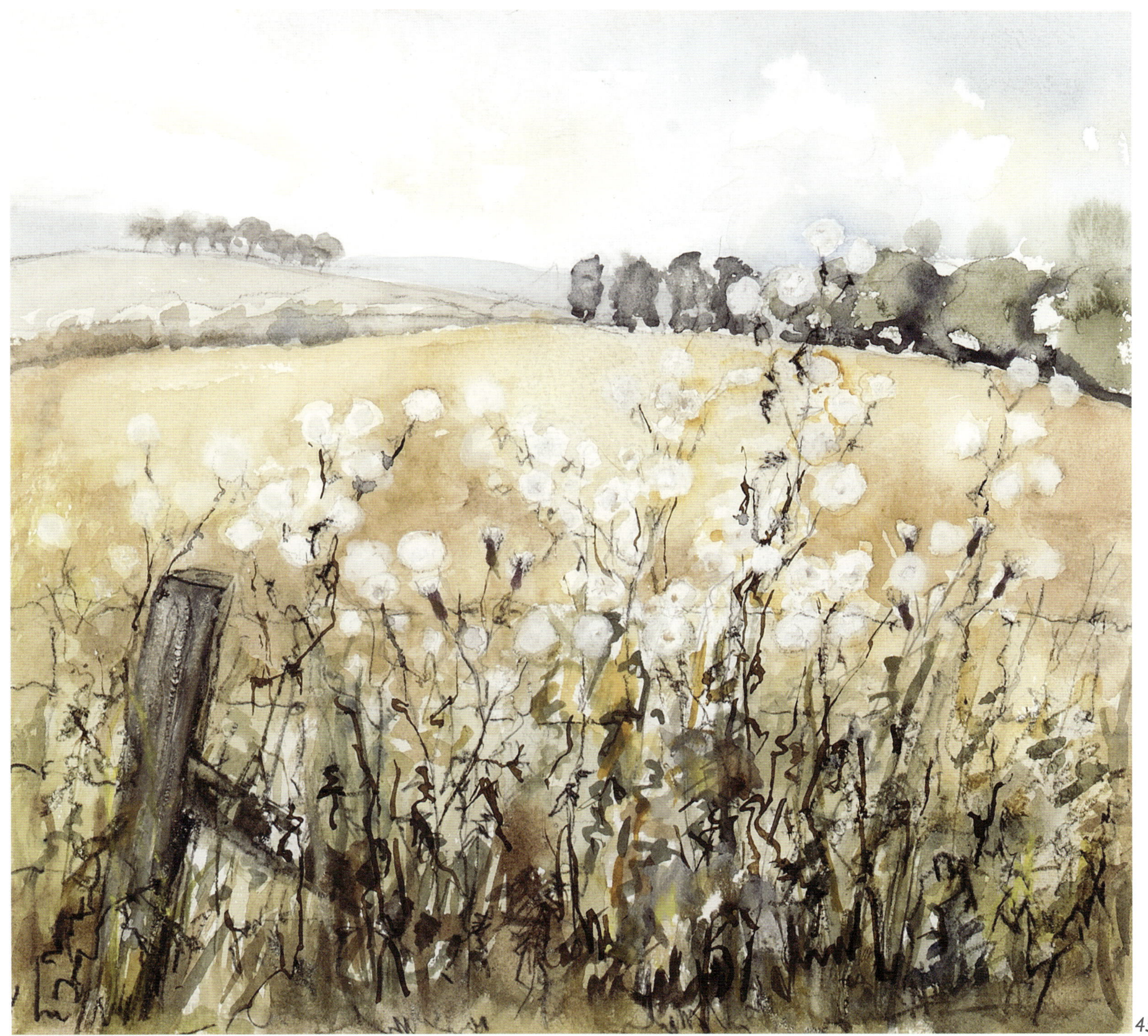

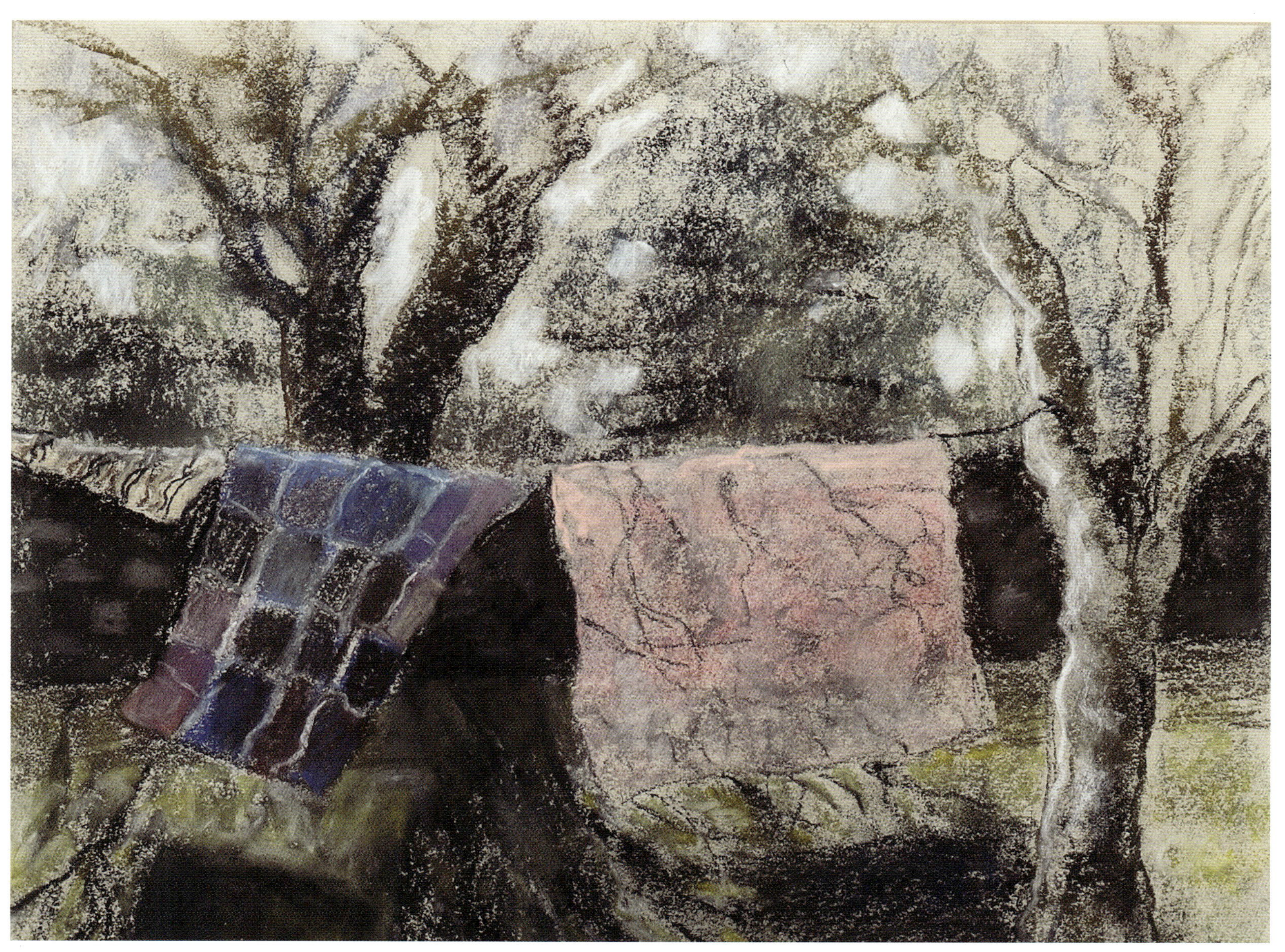

chalk 305 x 395mm

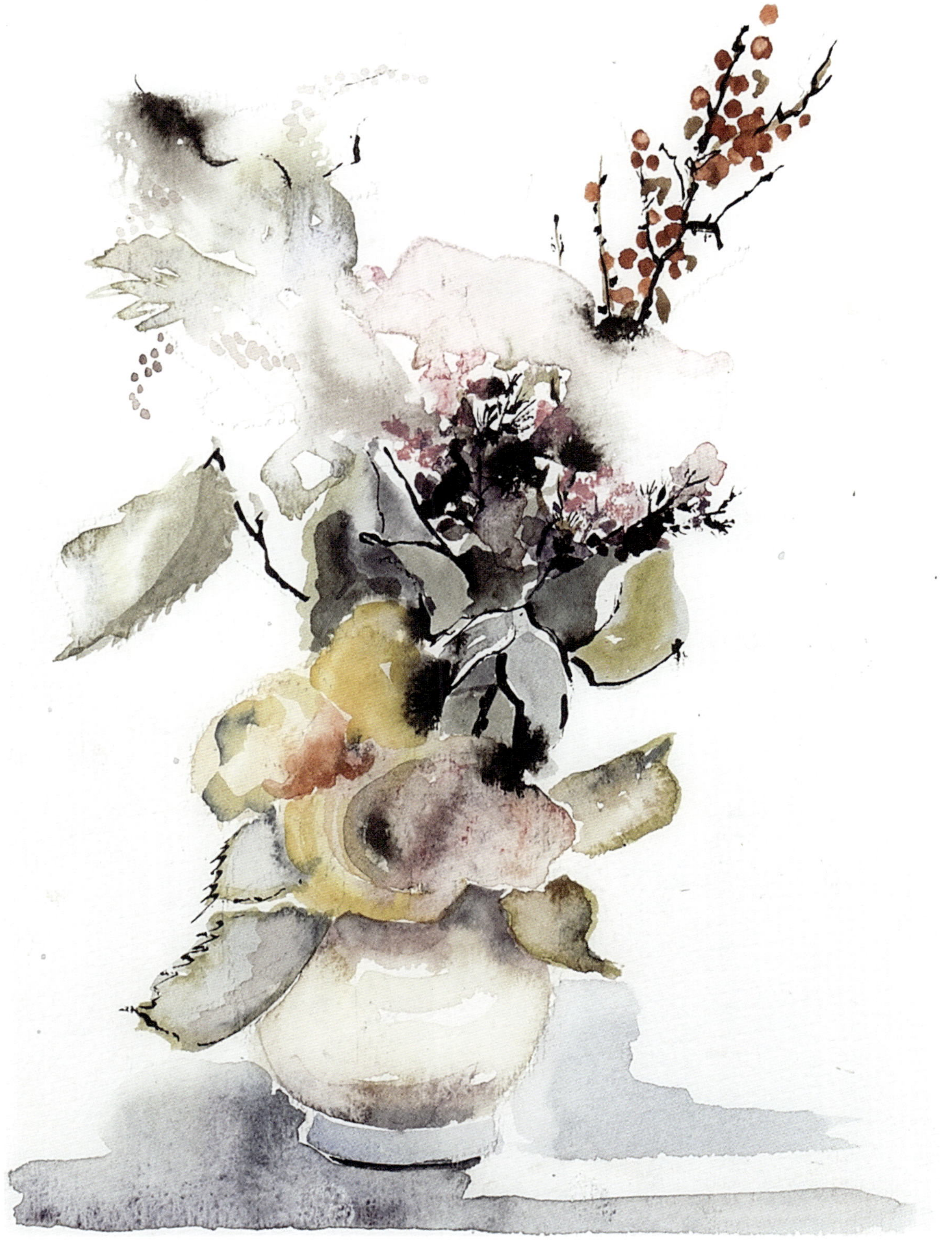

watercolour 282 x 216mm

Model in a Scarlet Fez

I can tell from your back:
the way you relax
into the chair's bowed curve,
your fringed yellow coat
thrown over it, creased
with careless ease;
from the leisurely angle
of one leg slung over the other,
foot thrusting into space,
and the tilt of your head
with its lush black hair
sporting that scarlet fez,
its tassel tantalising the air –
I can – I can tell you're smiling.
I certainly am! There's an invitation
in your open shirt collar – I'm sure
I can smell the roasted aroma
of Turkish coffee from a back-street café
where perhaps we'll meet to share thoughts
from that book you've brought,
its blood red cover vibrant as yourself.

pencil, ink and watercolour 565 x 345mm

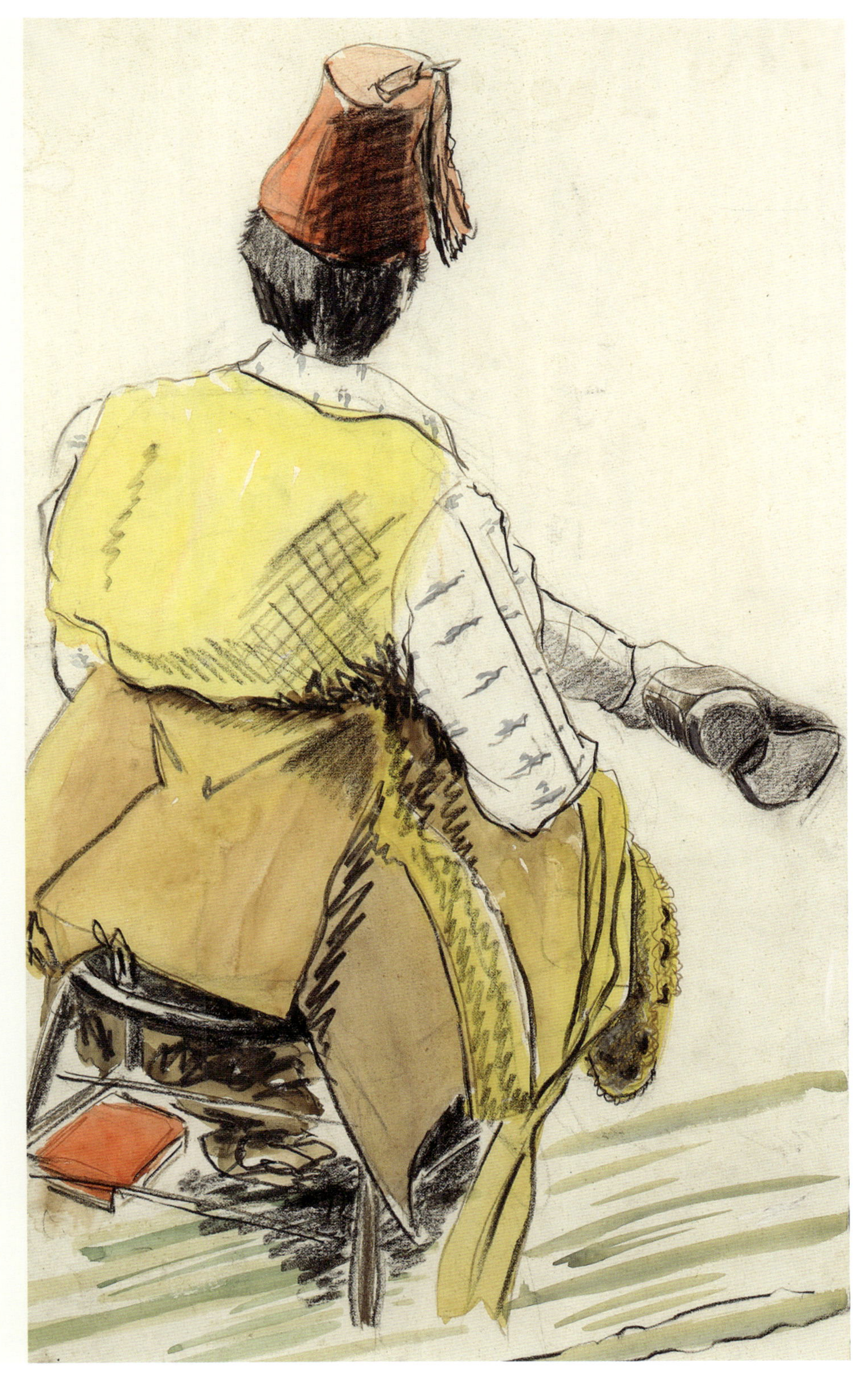

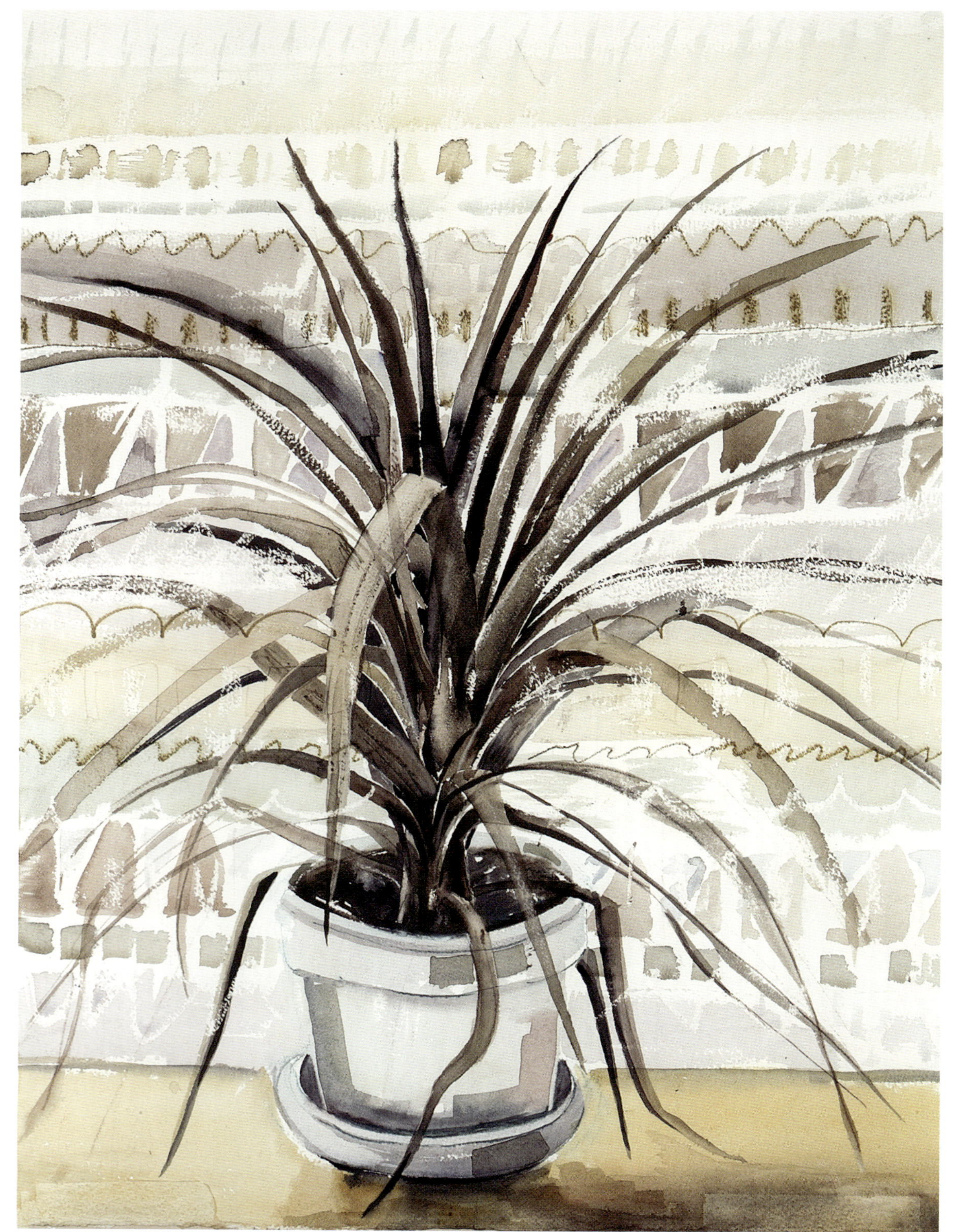

chalk and watercolour

650 x 495mm

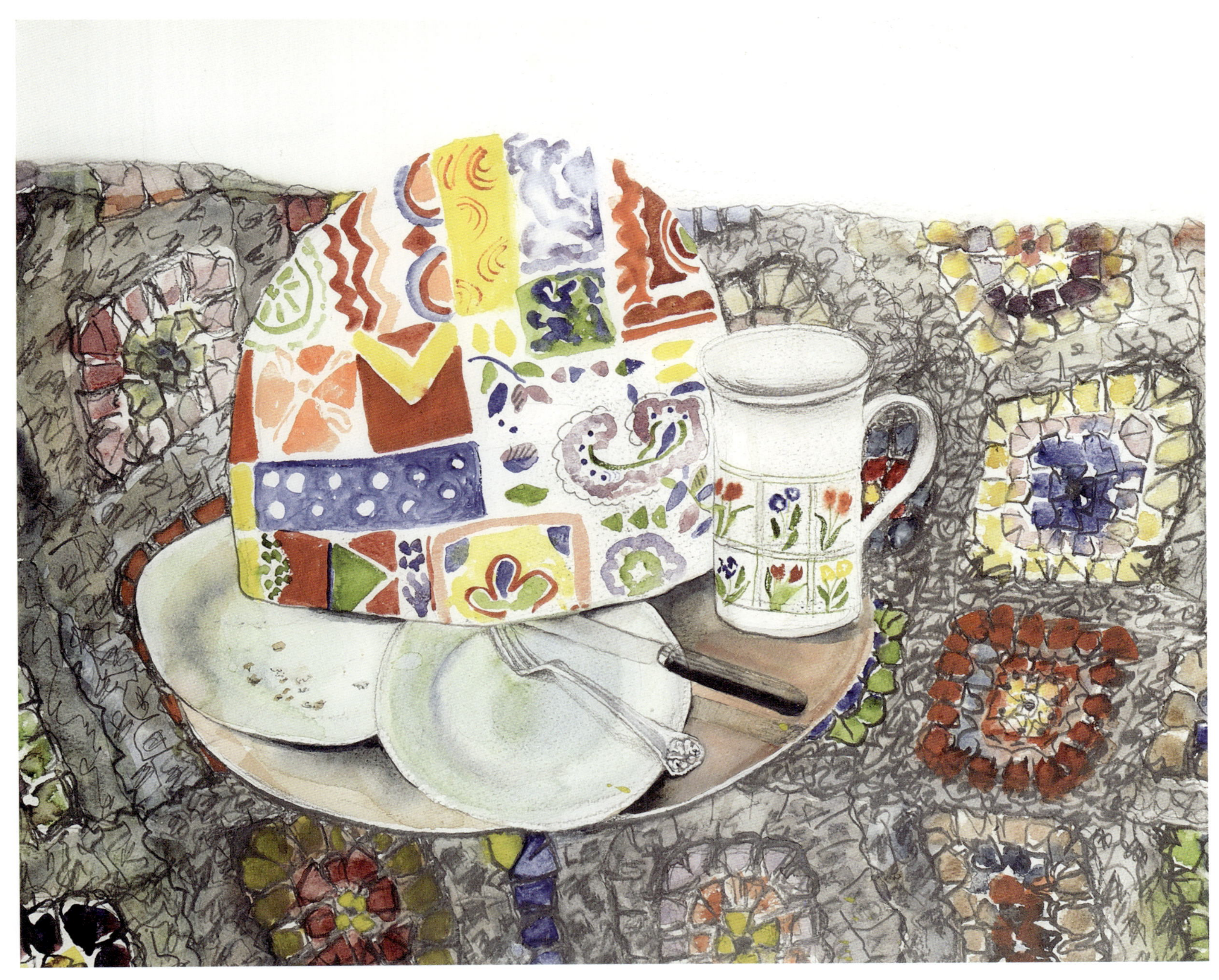

pencil and watercolour 420 x 510mm

51

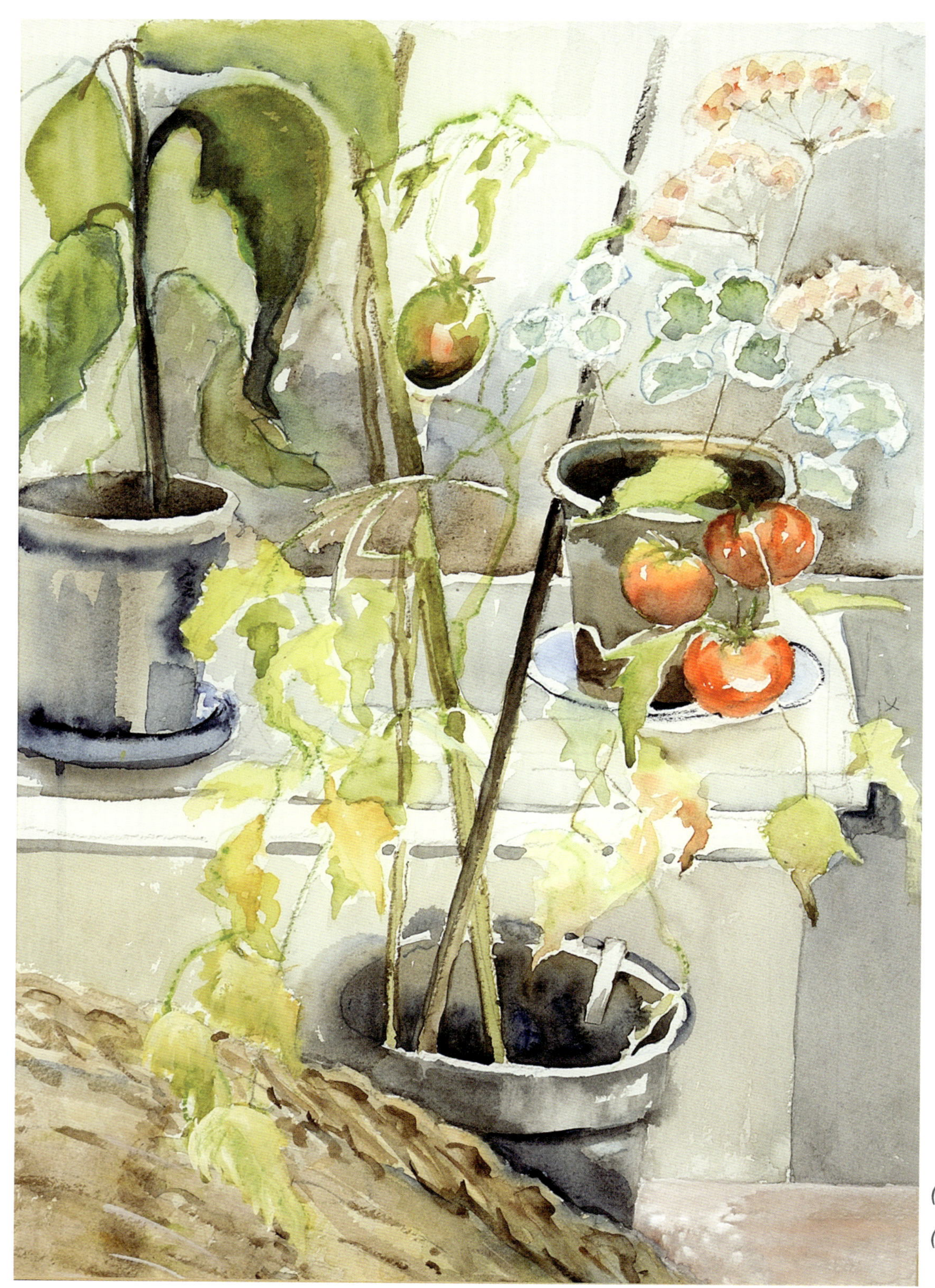

(left) watercolour 508 x 370mm

(opposite) watercolour 375 x 380mm

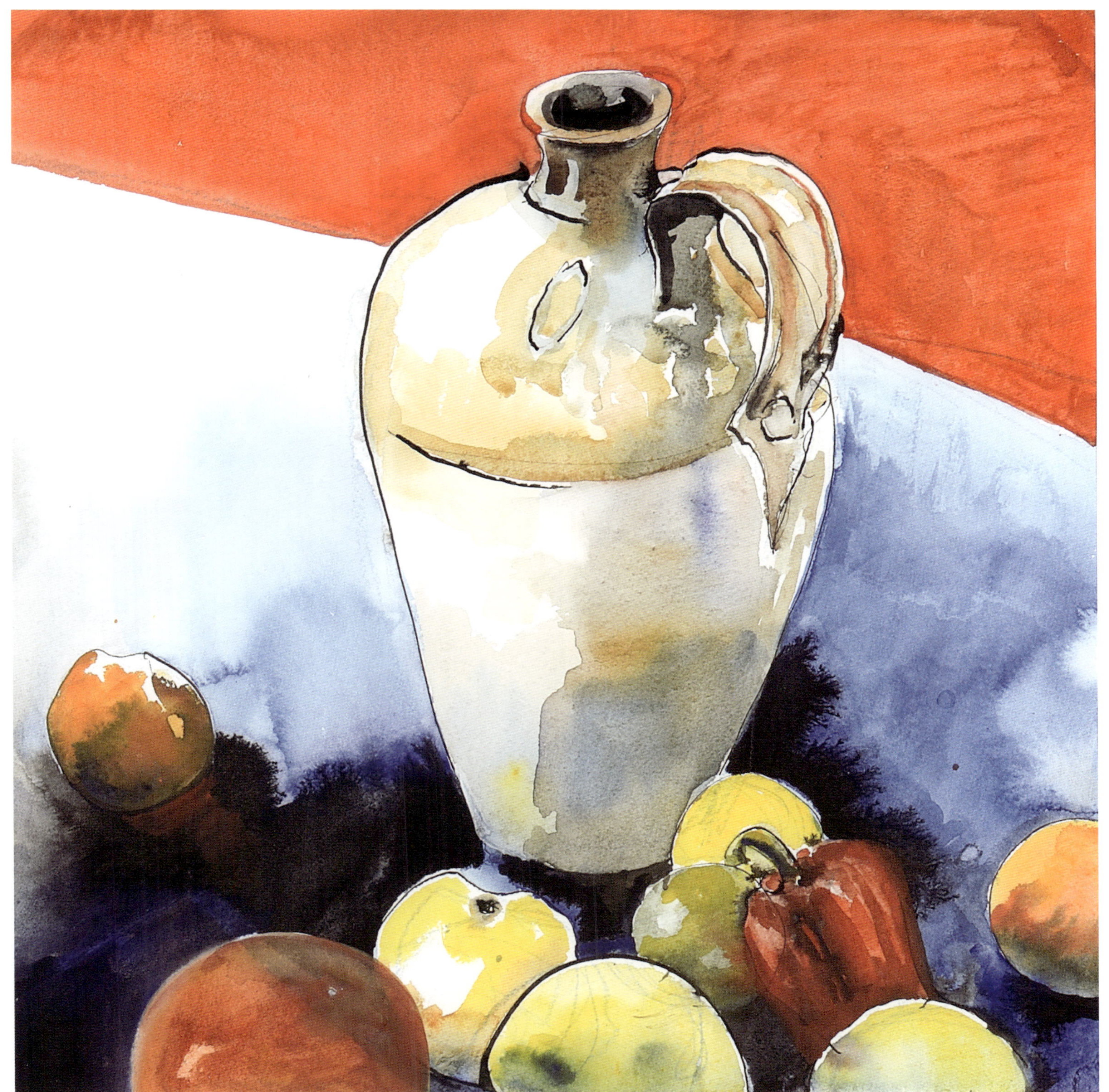

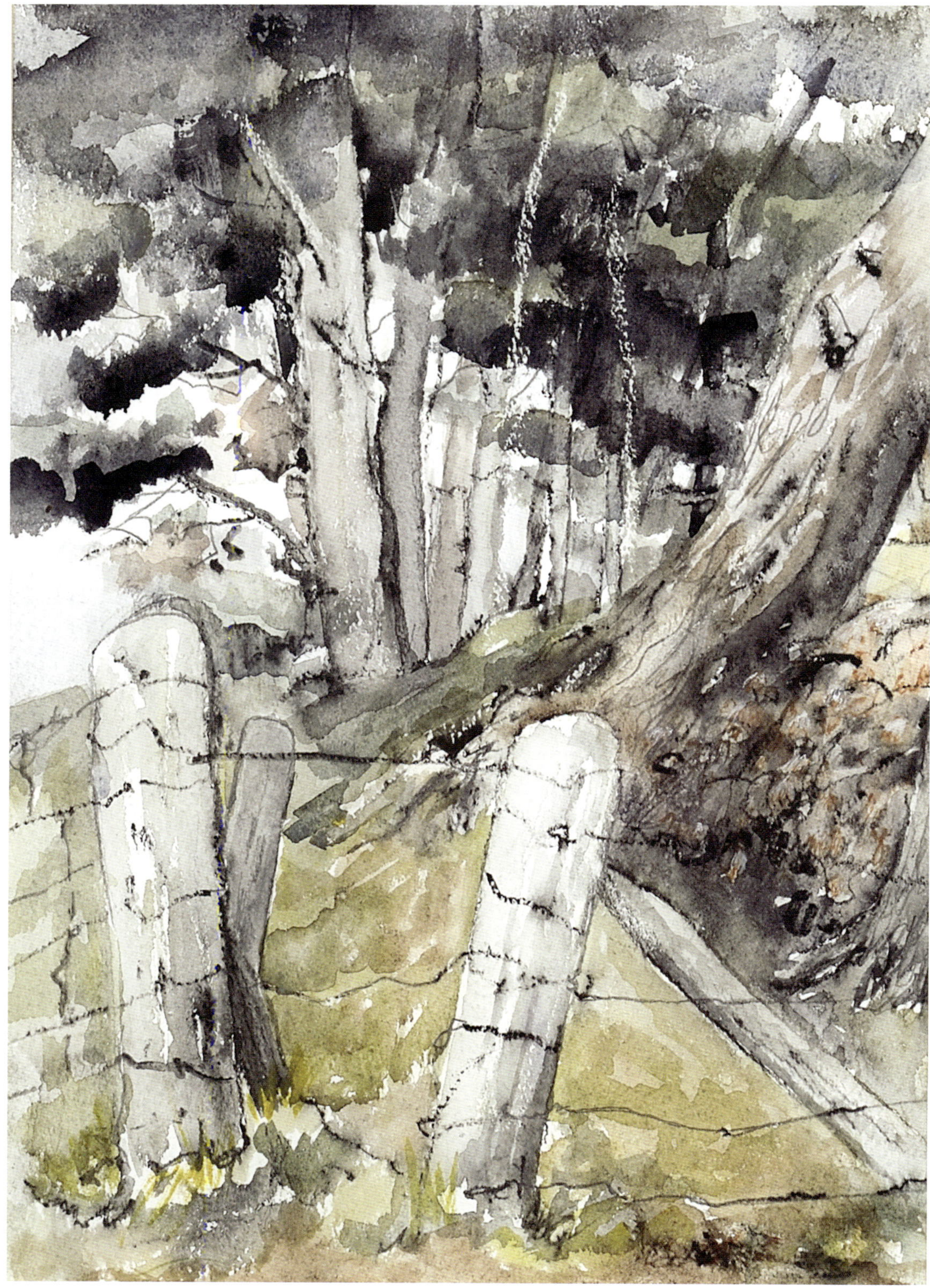

"The children have grown up and left home – I return and go further. I am free to walk alone now, unencumbered, though a happy encumbrance it was. I can carry my sketchbook and paints; peace to look closely at what warms my heart, absorbs me, makes me think. I revisit the old places, but go further, to explore the near horizons without limitation. I love this place, its gentle slopes, and distant views. I feel at home, and observe man's imprint on the land: stone walls, gate posts, fences. Many have been here before me. The pines edging Pirndean; the knarled roots of those ancient beeches above Tarfhaugh; the pines encompassing the old fort on Henderland Hill above Callands; a crow hung on barbed wire – the same tribe that killed moles and hung them on fences? We are cruel."

watercolour 325 x 236mm

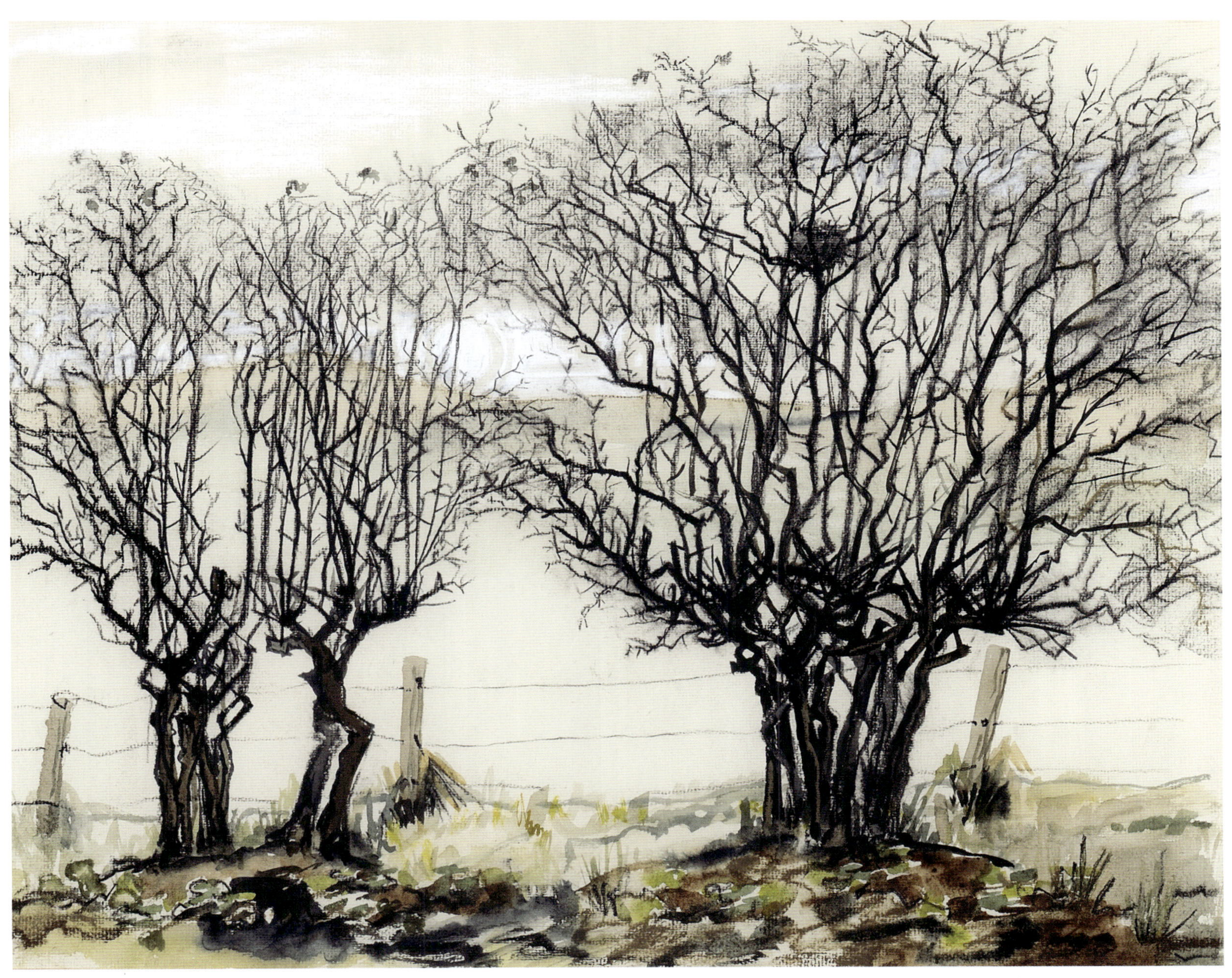

watercolour, charcoal and ink 355 x 455mm

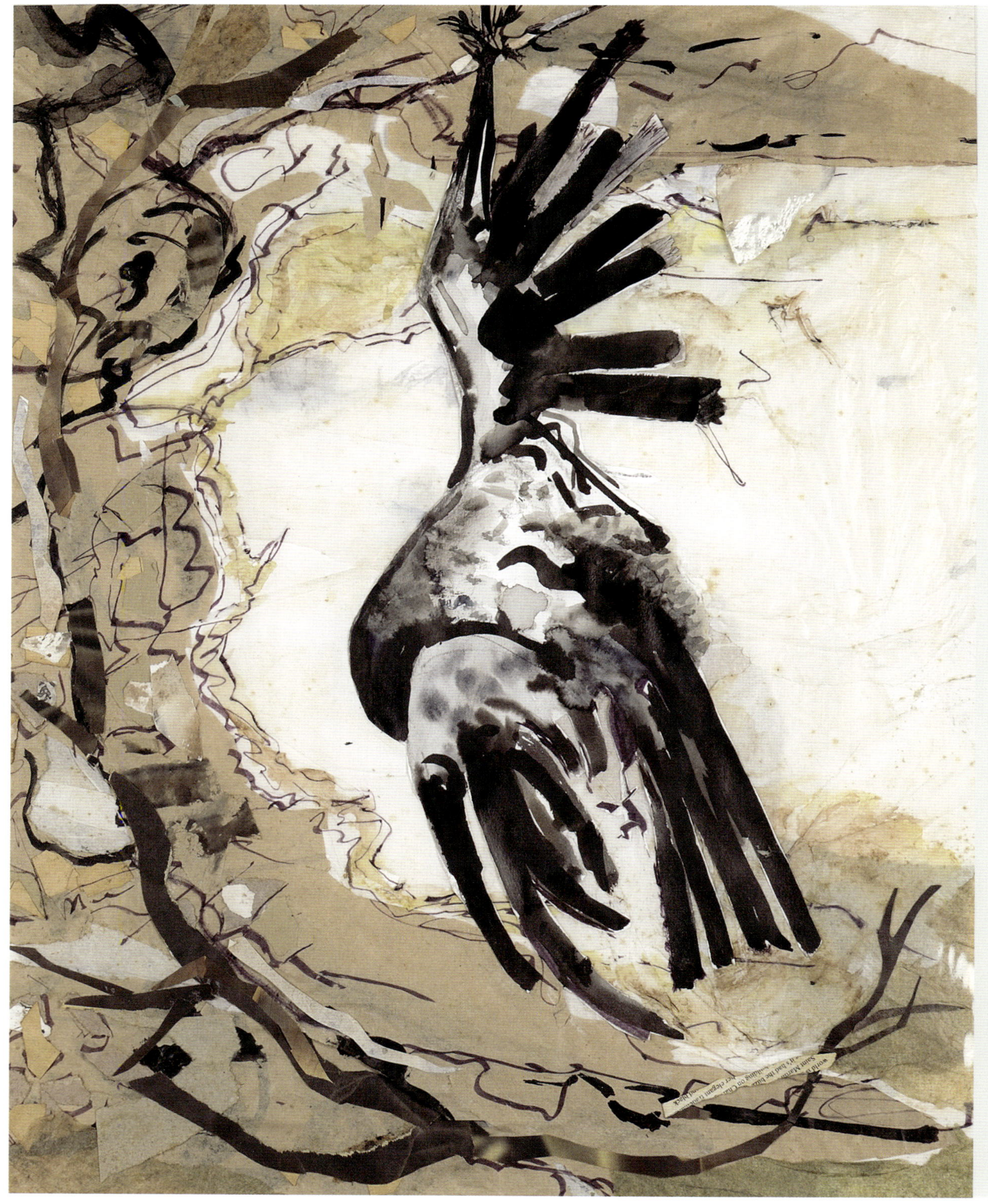

Crow

I don't paint death and decay, but today -
my mind, prey to the sudden way dark things
can snare me in broad daylight – I face my fear,
nail it to paper with a black rage
that wild grace could be so slayed –
the dead, lead weight hanging there,
from one fanned wing on a single barb,
the heartbreak downward sweep
of head bowed to ground, emblem of defeat,
pinned to the white air.

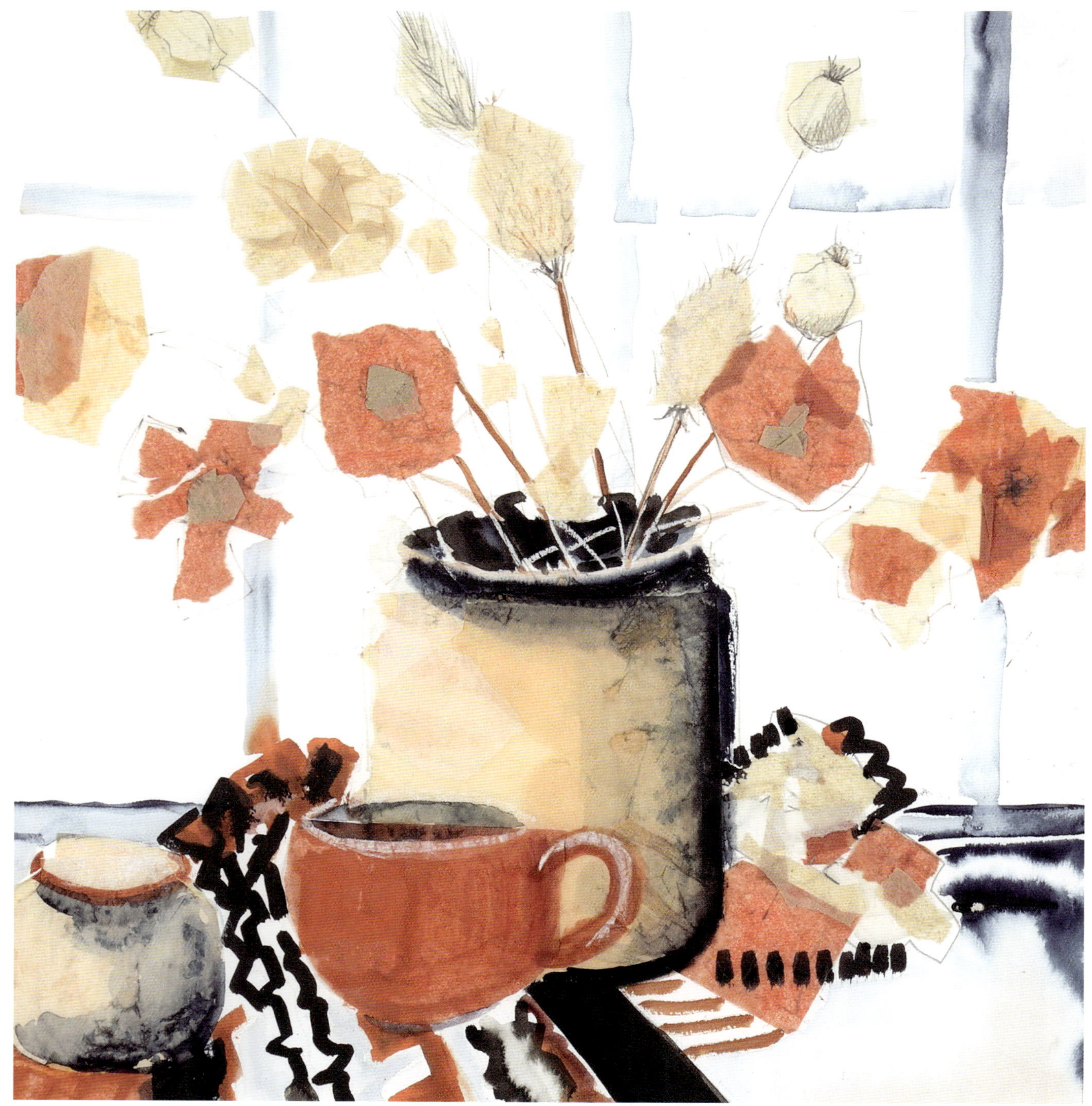

watercolour with tissue paper, 506 x 449mm

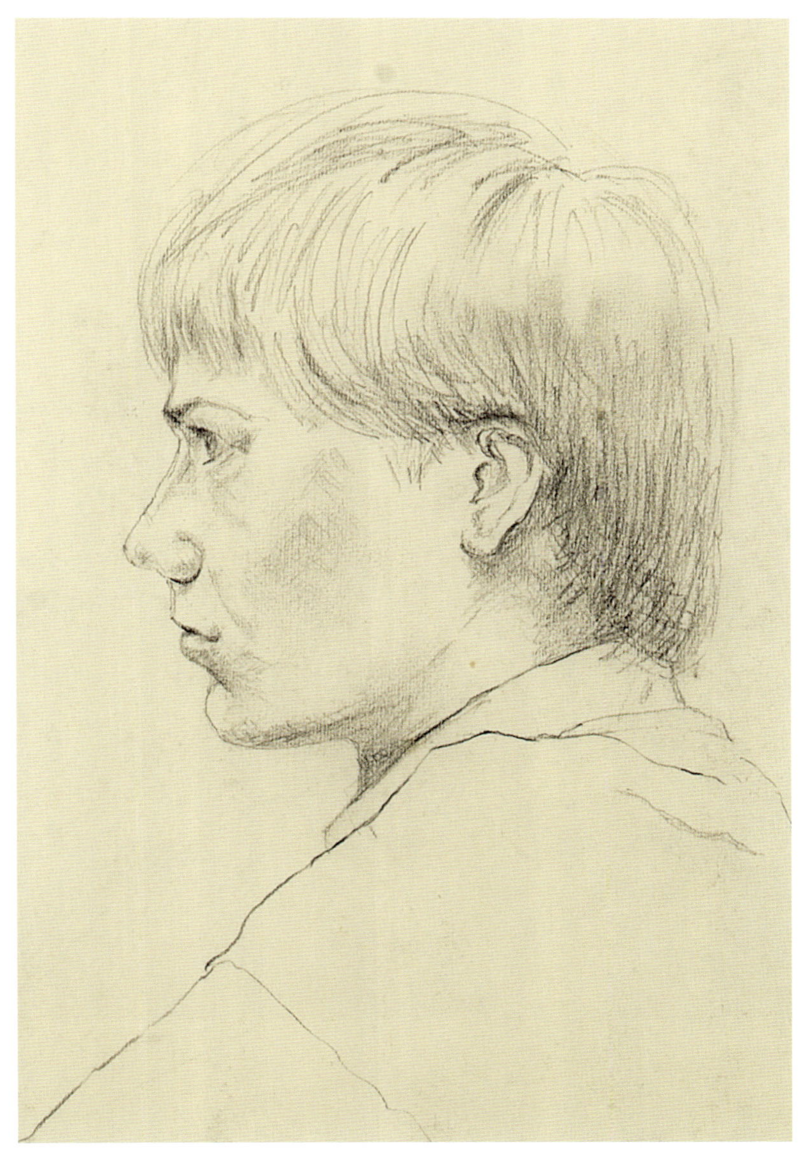

pencil 340 x 270mm

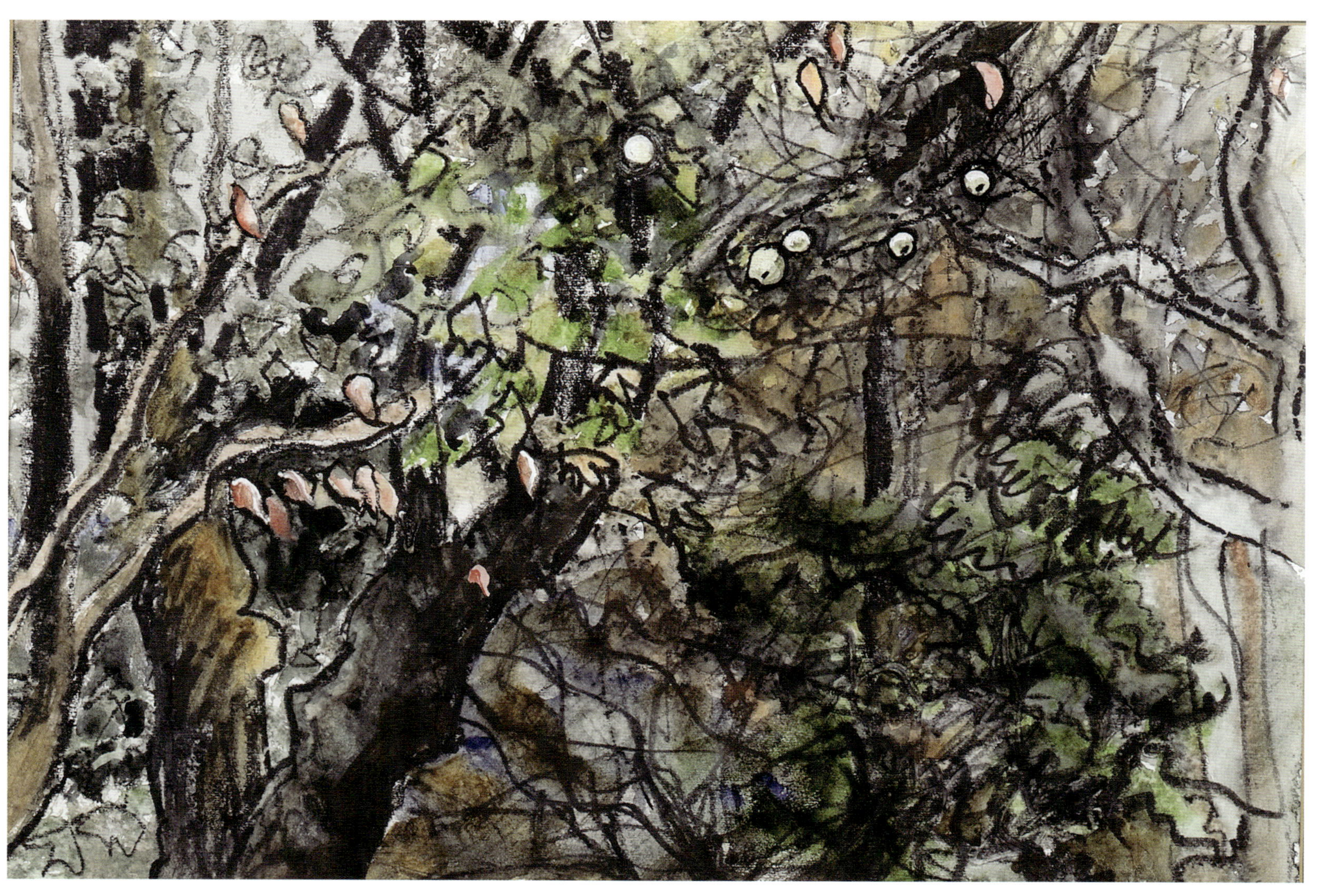

watercolour and charcoal 295 x 445mm

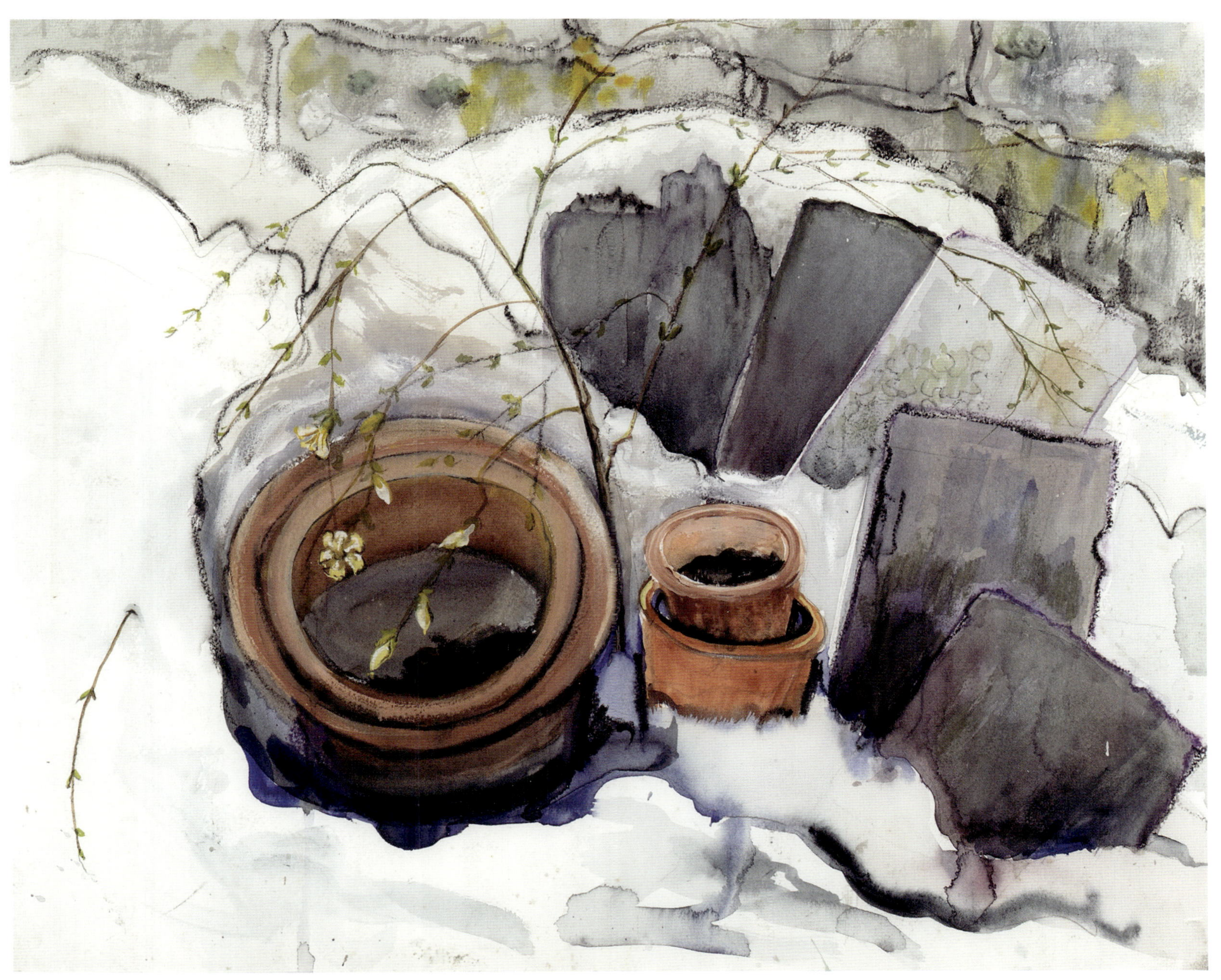

watercolour and charcoal 420 x 504mm

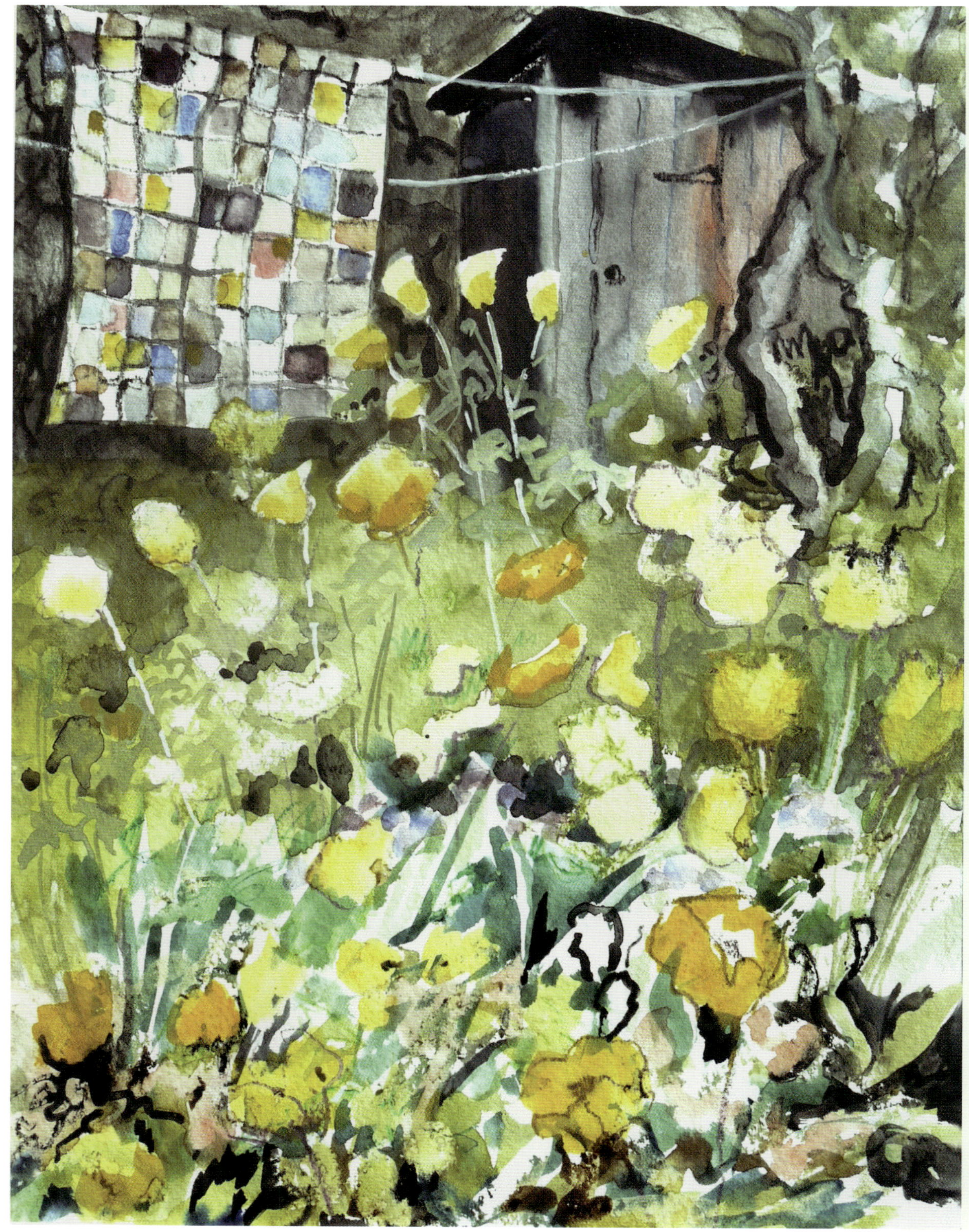

watercolour 297 x232mm

Patchwork Quilt

So many days hang on the washing line
in the stillness of this summer afternoon,
remnants of childhood that once flickered
across the village green – polka dots,
stripes and checks, the good parts retained
and reframed for service in a second life
here in my mother's home, where my footsteps
shuffle in the ghost of hers; I know so well
who wore each square, and when –
those laughing times stitched onto memory
in sharp lines; but today I'll place them
as a backdrop, their detail indistinct,
an echo only of the here and now, where blossoms
mother planted dazzle my eye with their own
random patchwork, and distract from the bruised tones
of the garden shed that stands sentinel by the wall,
waiting to hold court when winter falls.

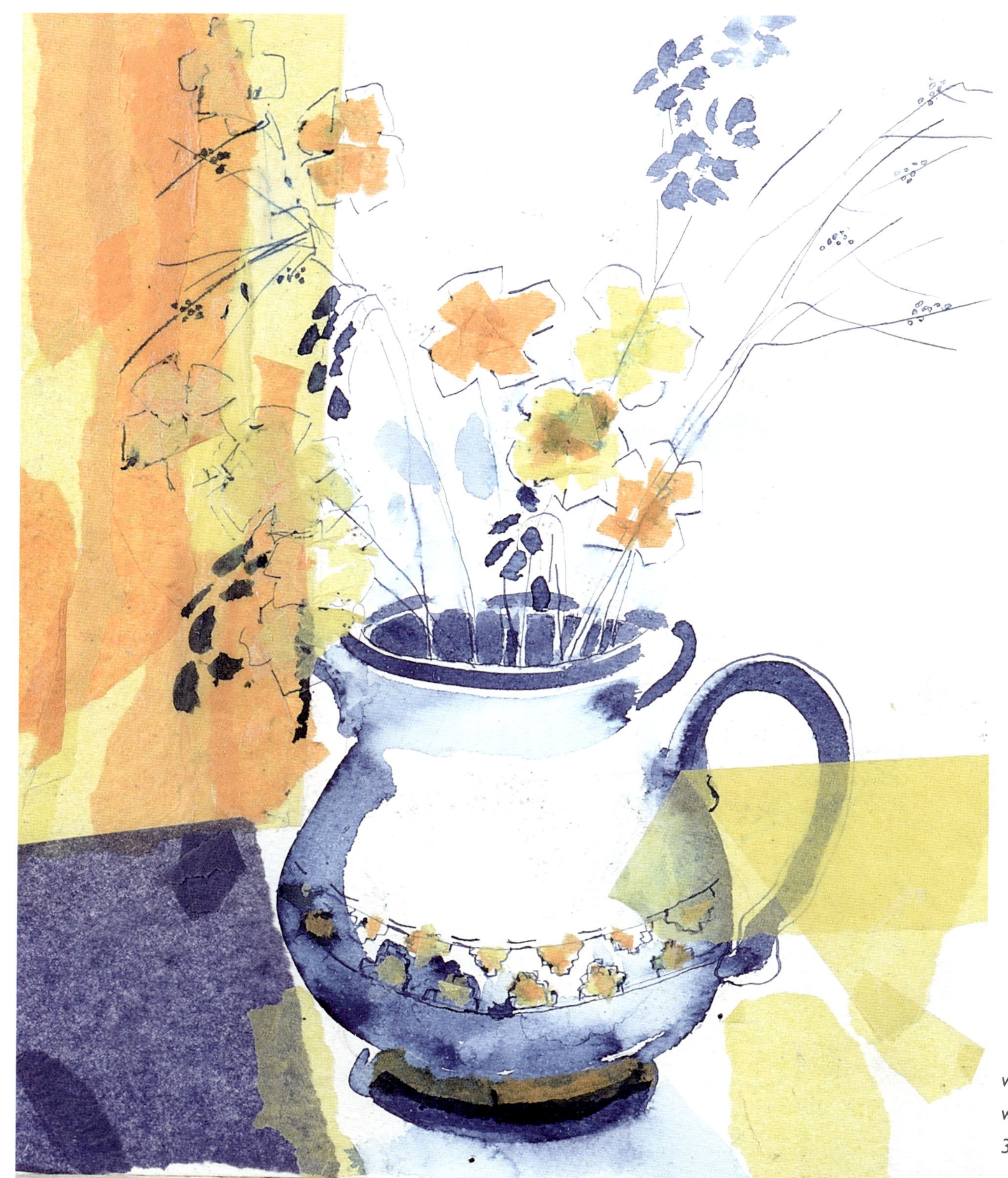

*watercolour and ink
with tissue paper
350 x 295mm*

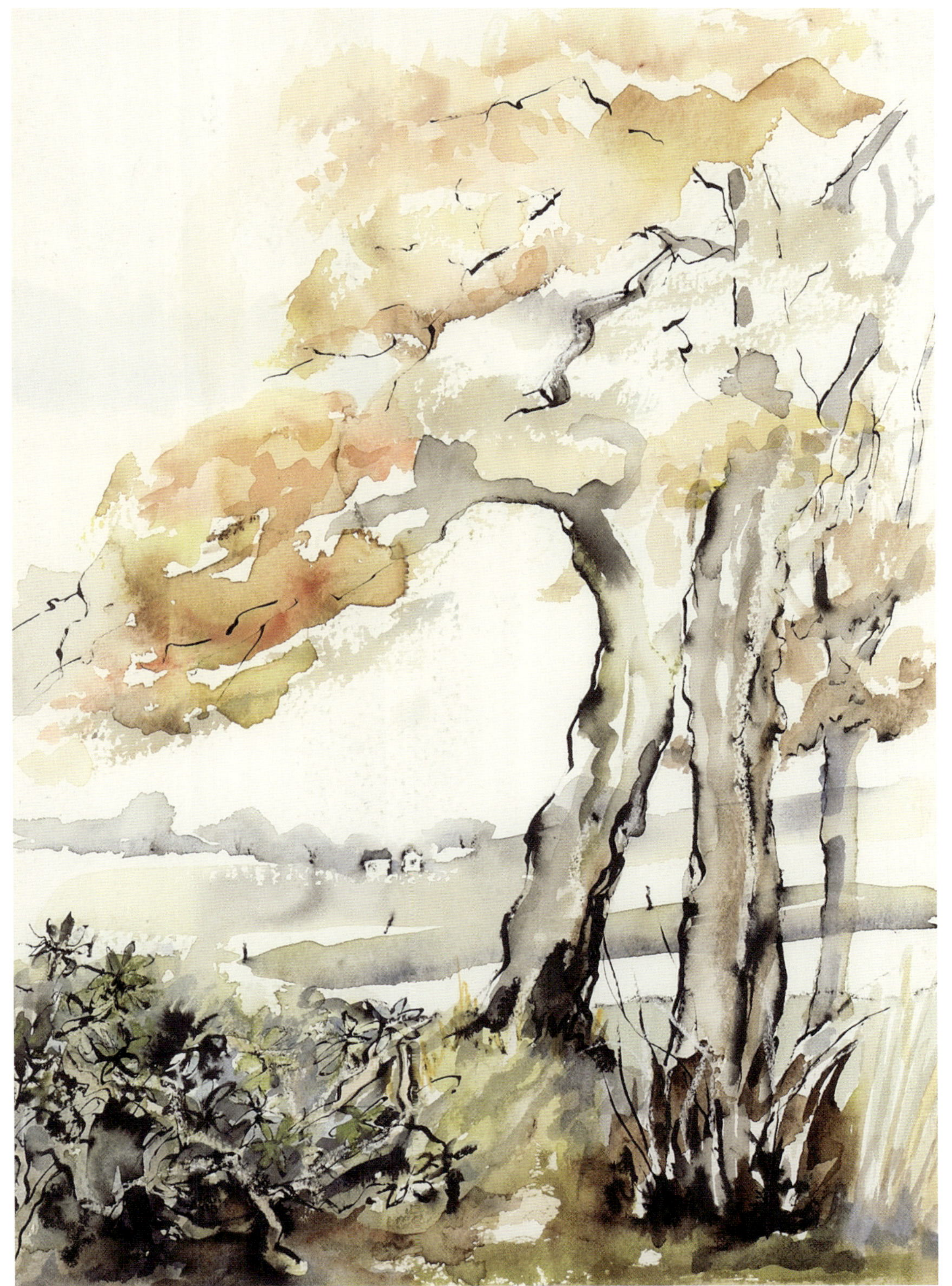

watercolour
315 x 400mm

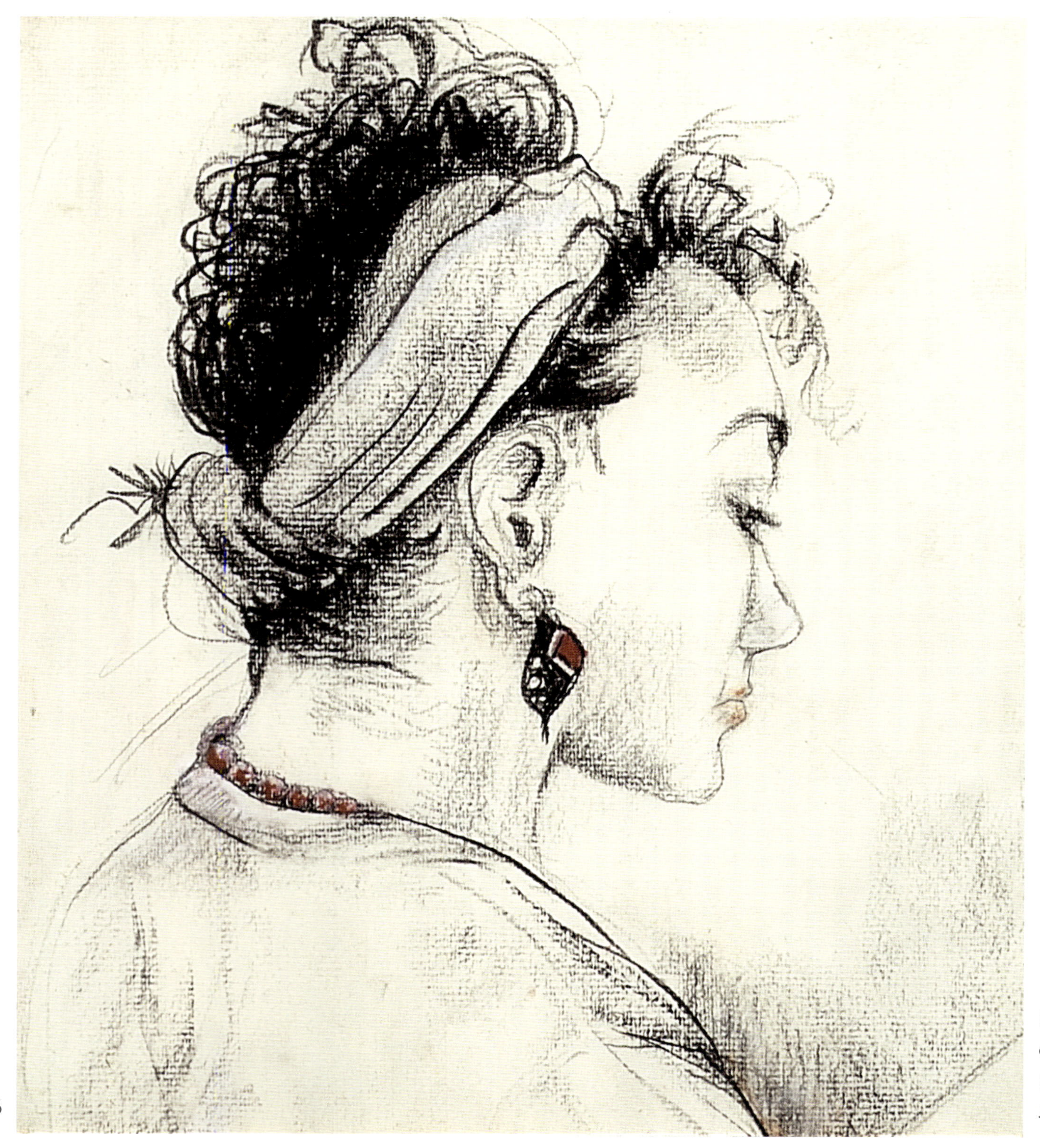

(left) charcoal and
chalk 235 x 210mm
(opposite) watercolour
300 x 350mm

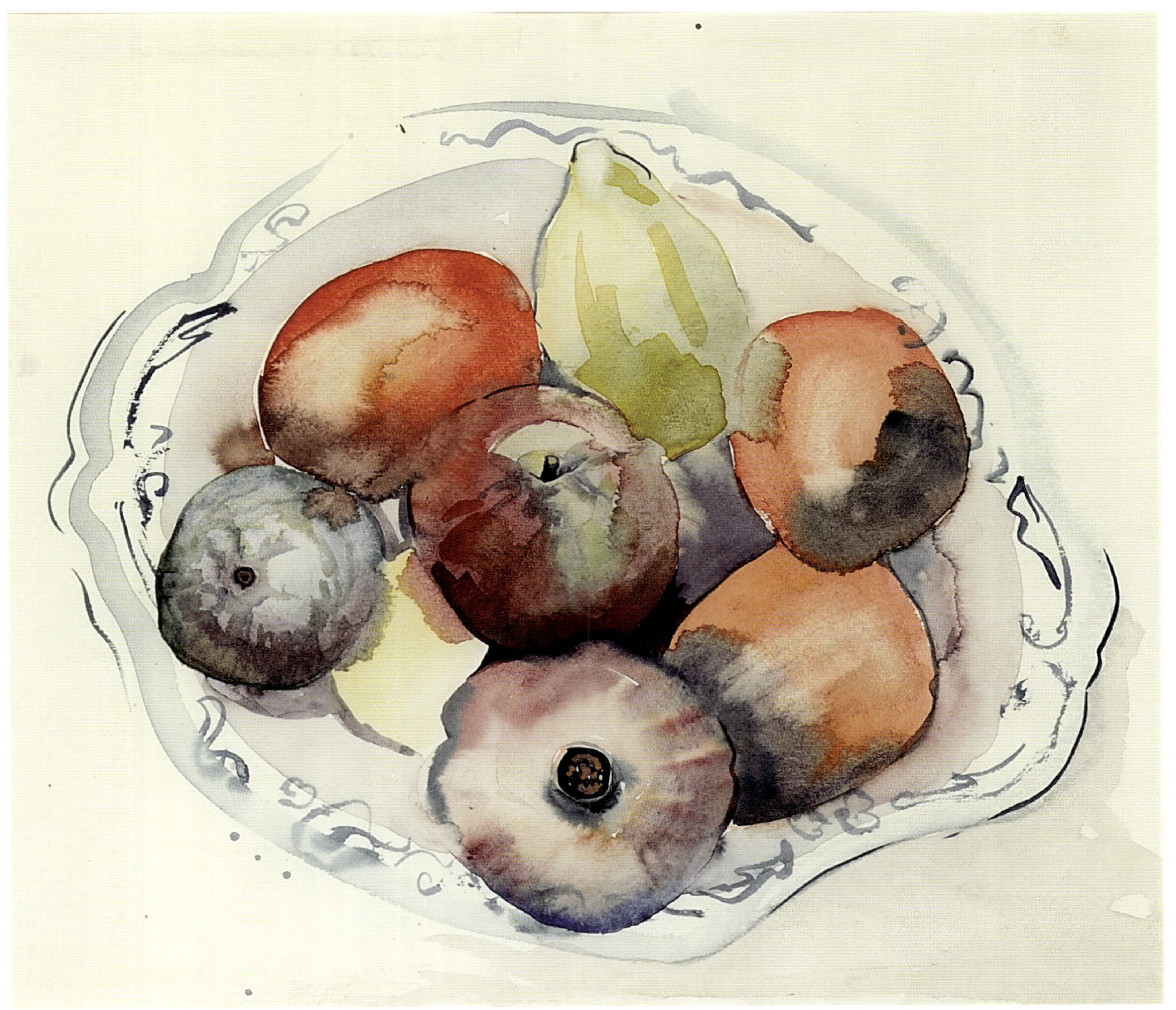

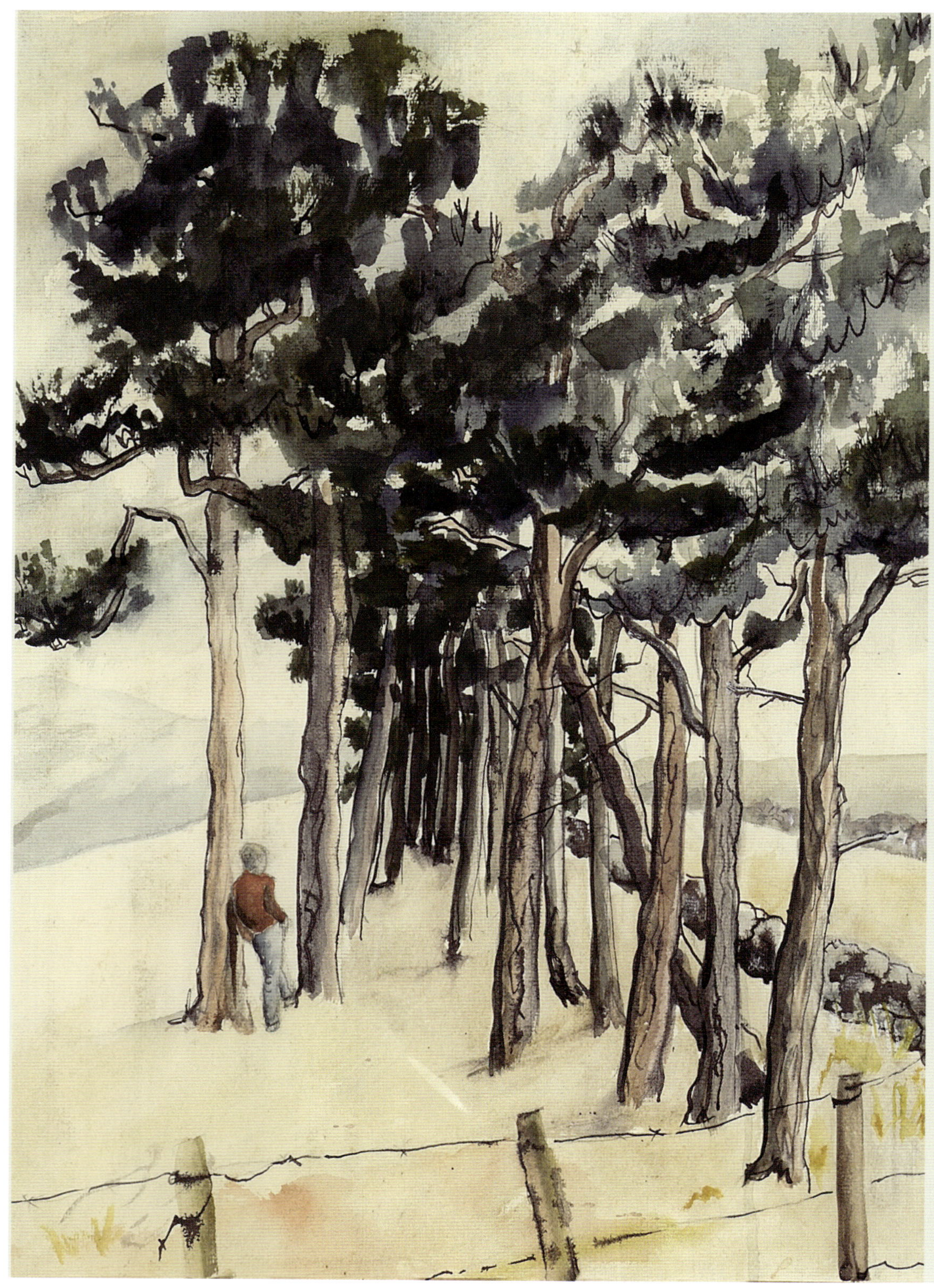

watercolour 470 x 370mm

Boy among the Pines

Those old Caledonian pines
on winter hills bring comfort:
steadfast, evergreen,
they'll outlive us all;
so I'll place a boy there,
emblem of the ephemeral,
for my three living sons,
and the one who left too soon –
leaning solitary yet carefree
against the tallest tree,
dressed in red – a heart-beat
to animate the scene.

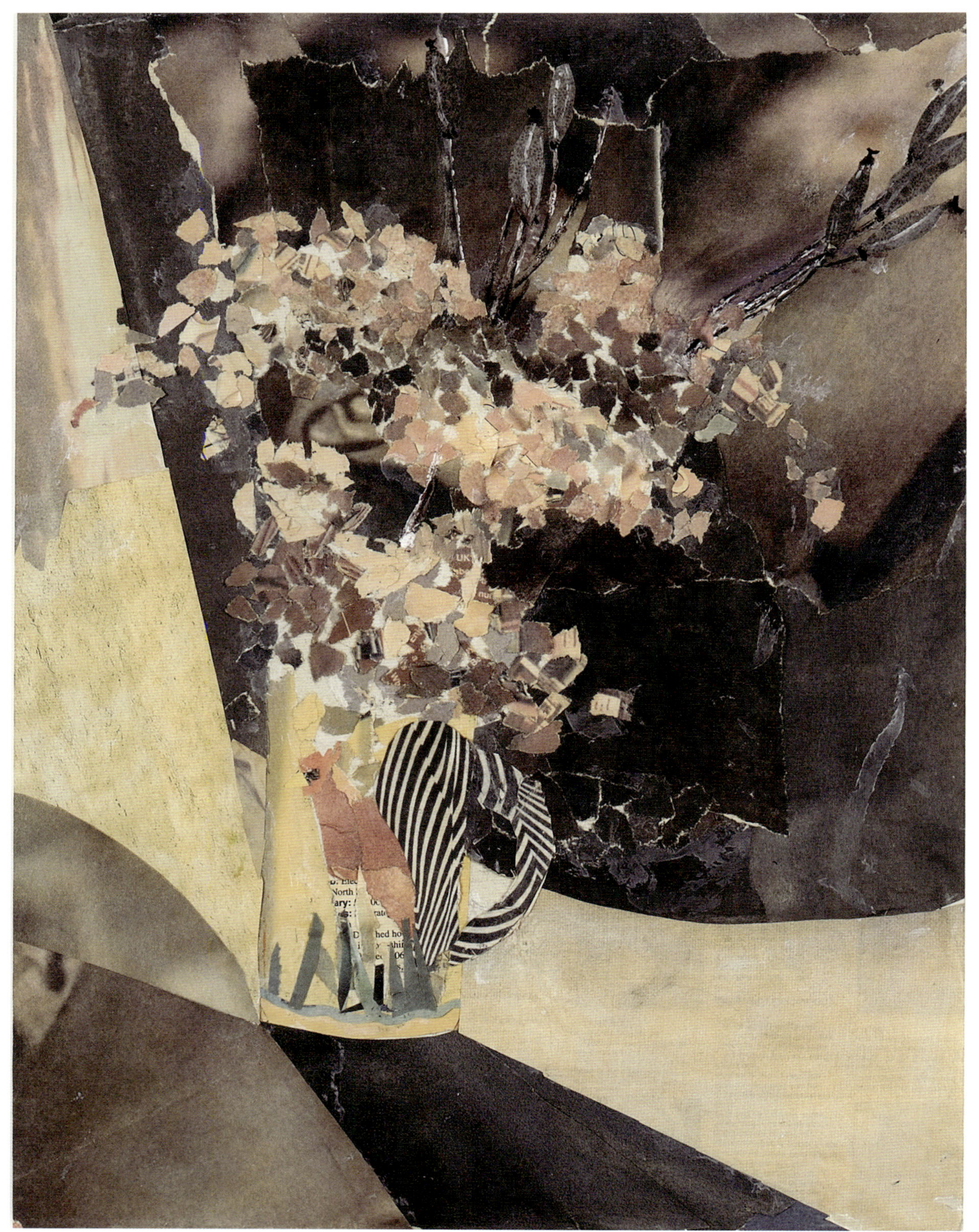

watercolour and paper collage

400 x 310mm

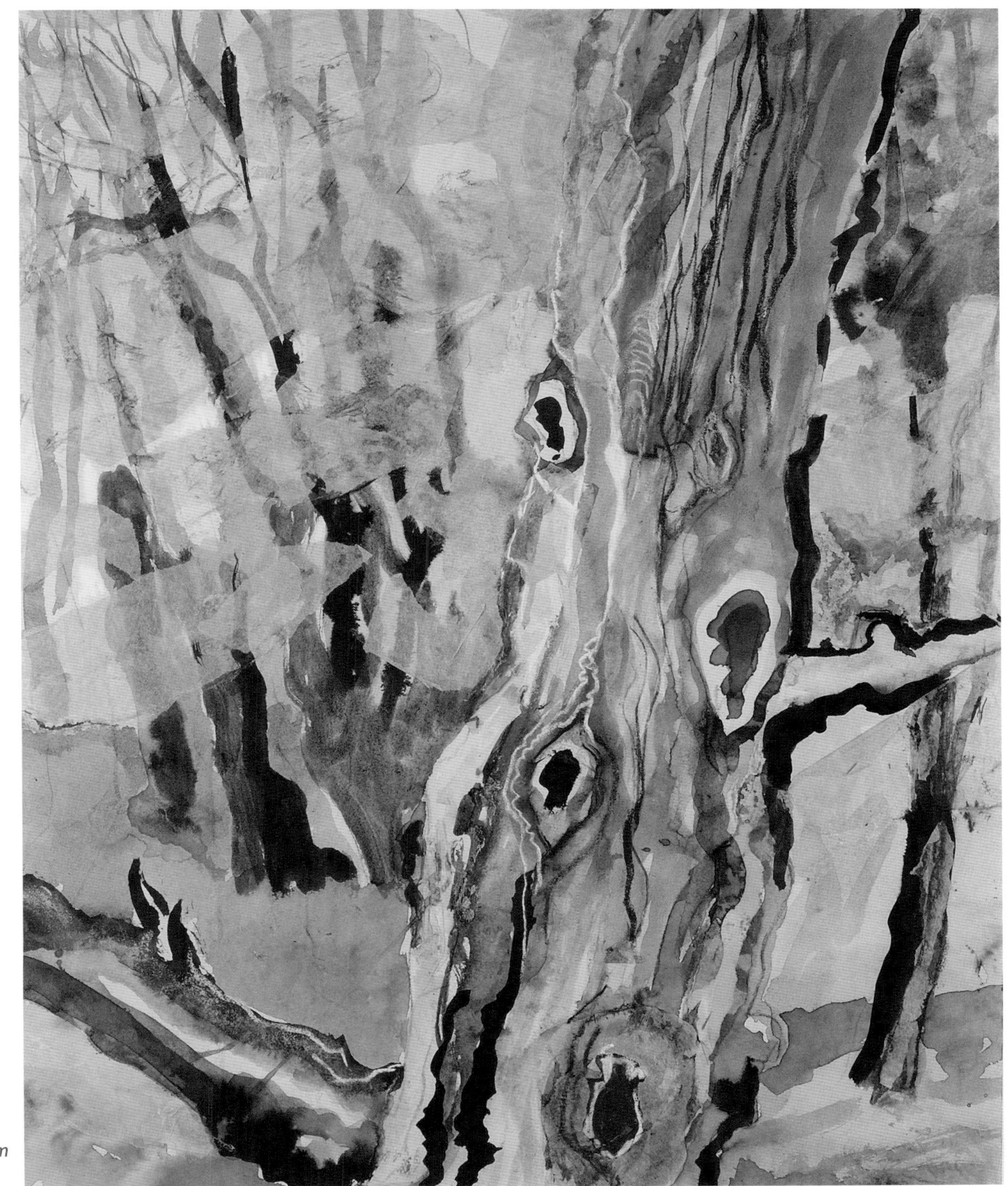

watercolour & chalk on
tissue paper 588 x 486mm

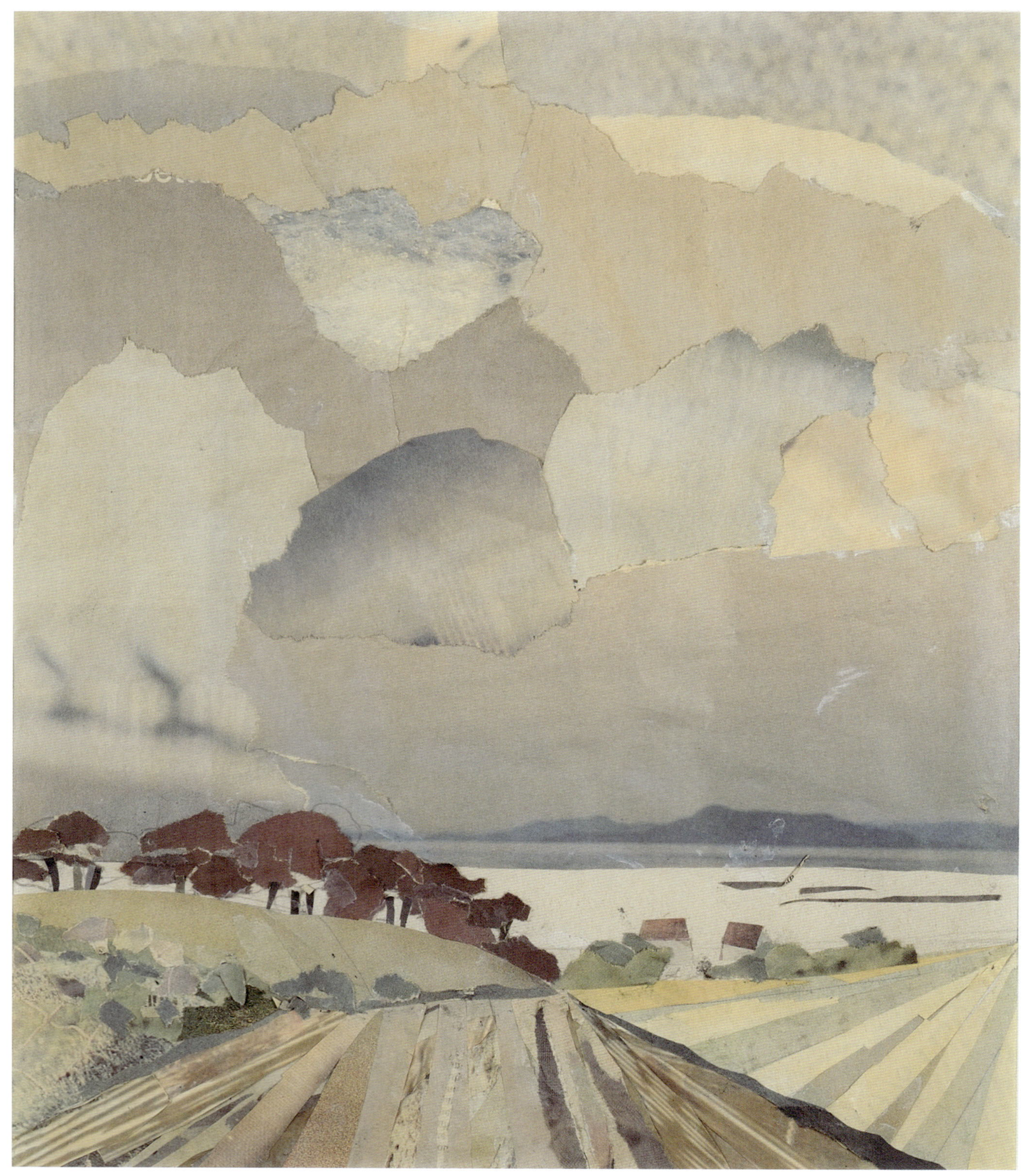

chalk on paper collage
330 x 290mm

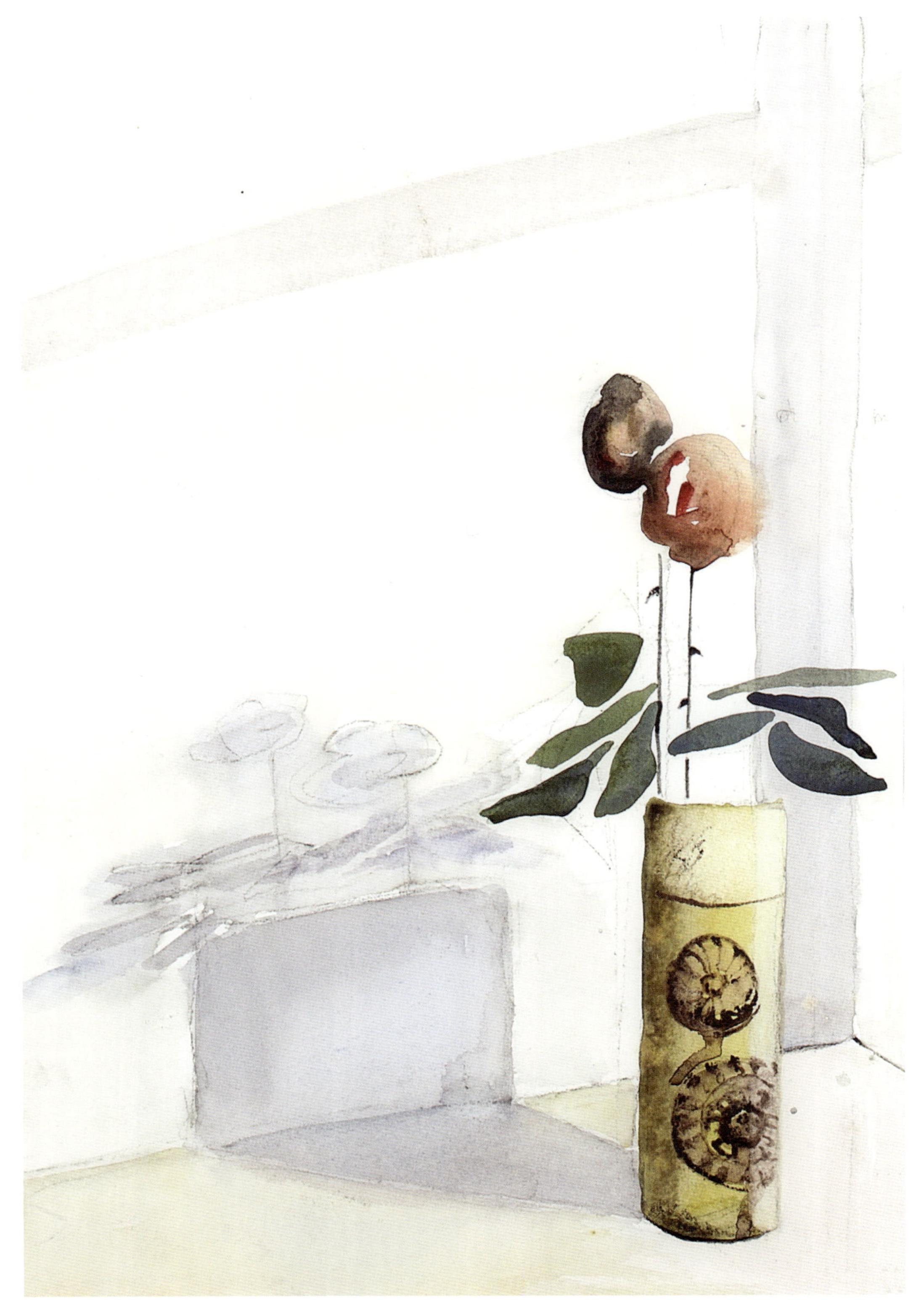

watercolour
405 x 208mm

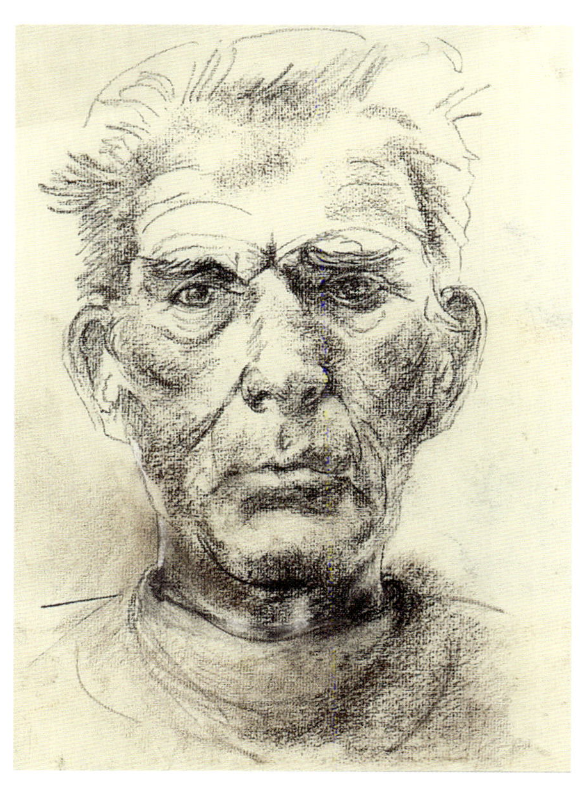

Kindling

Gathered sticks, cradled
in woven willow, wait
by my hearth – a promise of fire.
I'll render them in charcoal
before they wither to ash.

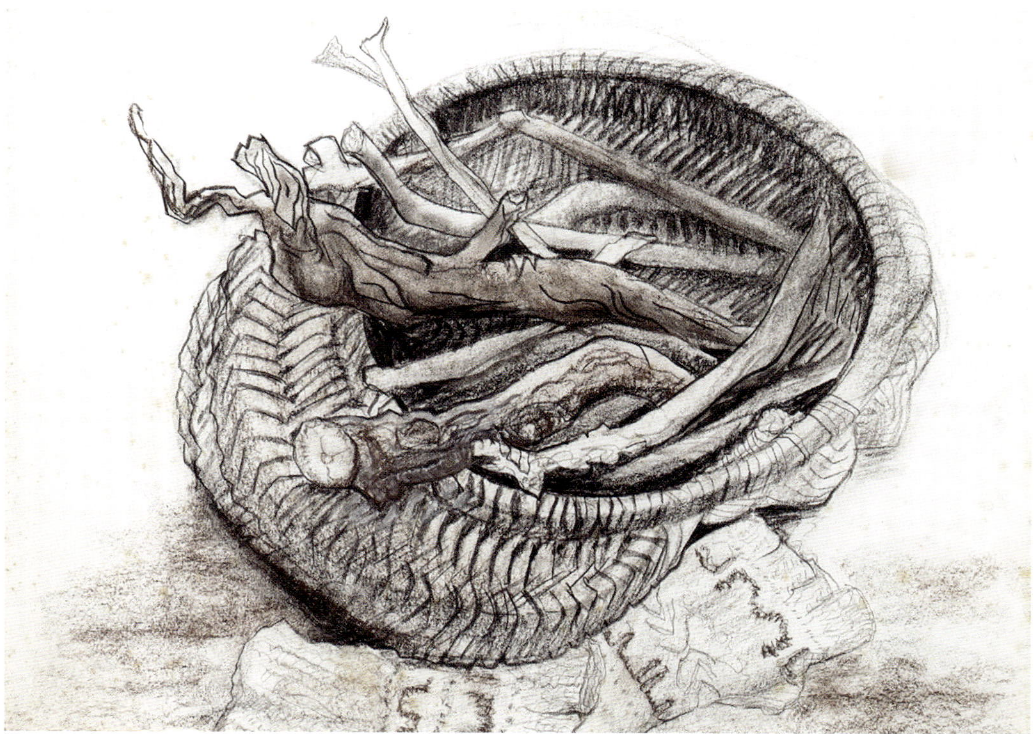

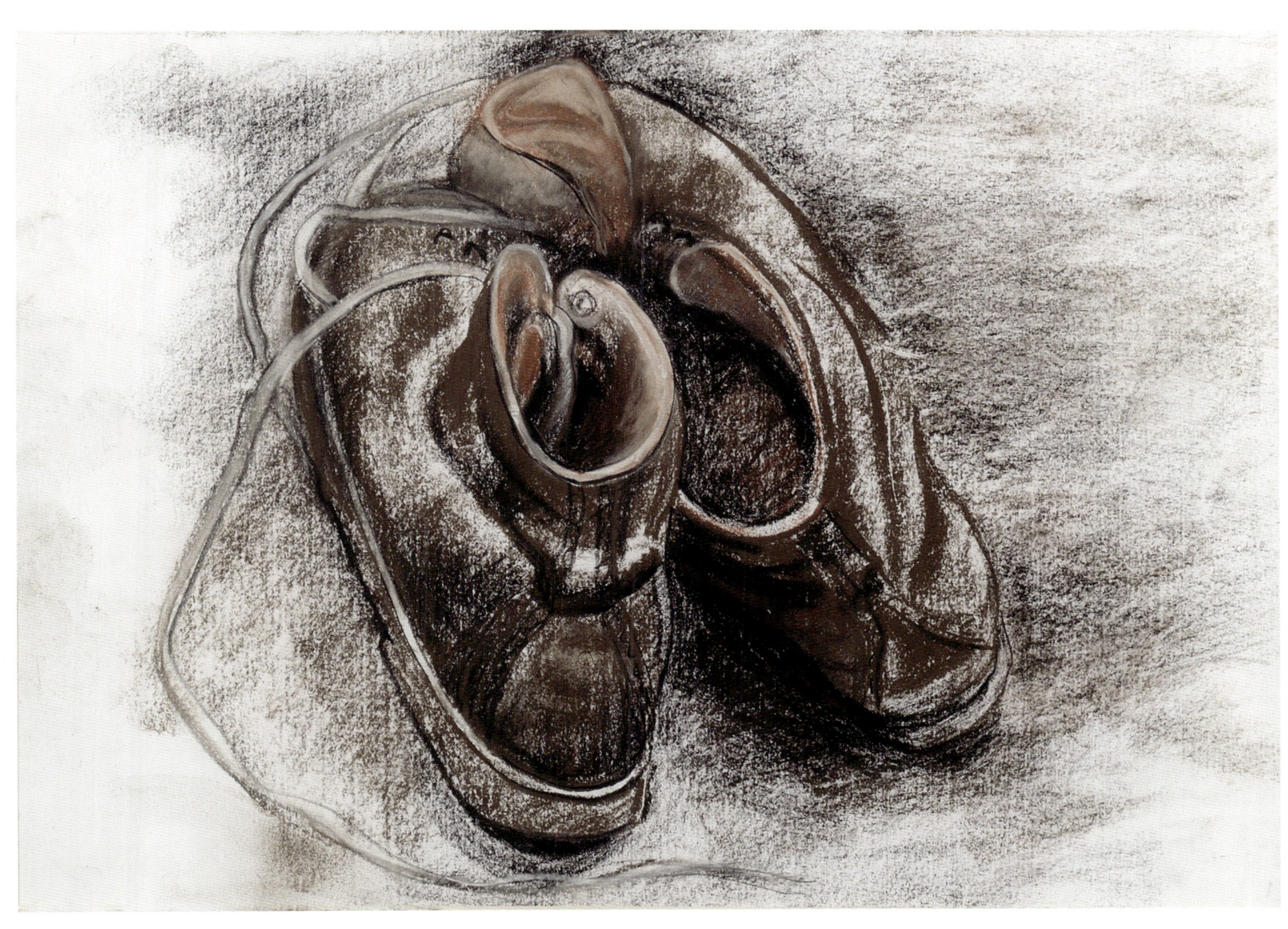

(opposite top) charcoal 400 x 310mm (opposite below) charcoal 285 x 410mm

(above) chalk 275 x 405mm

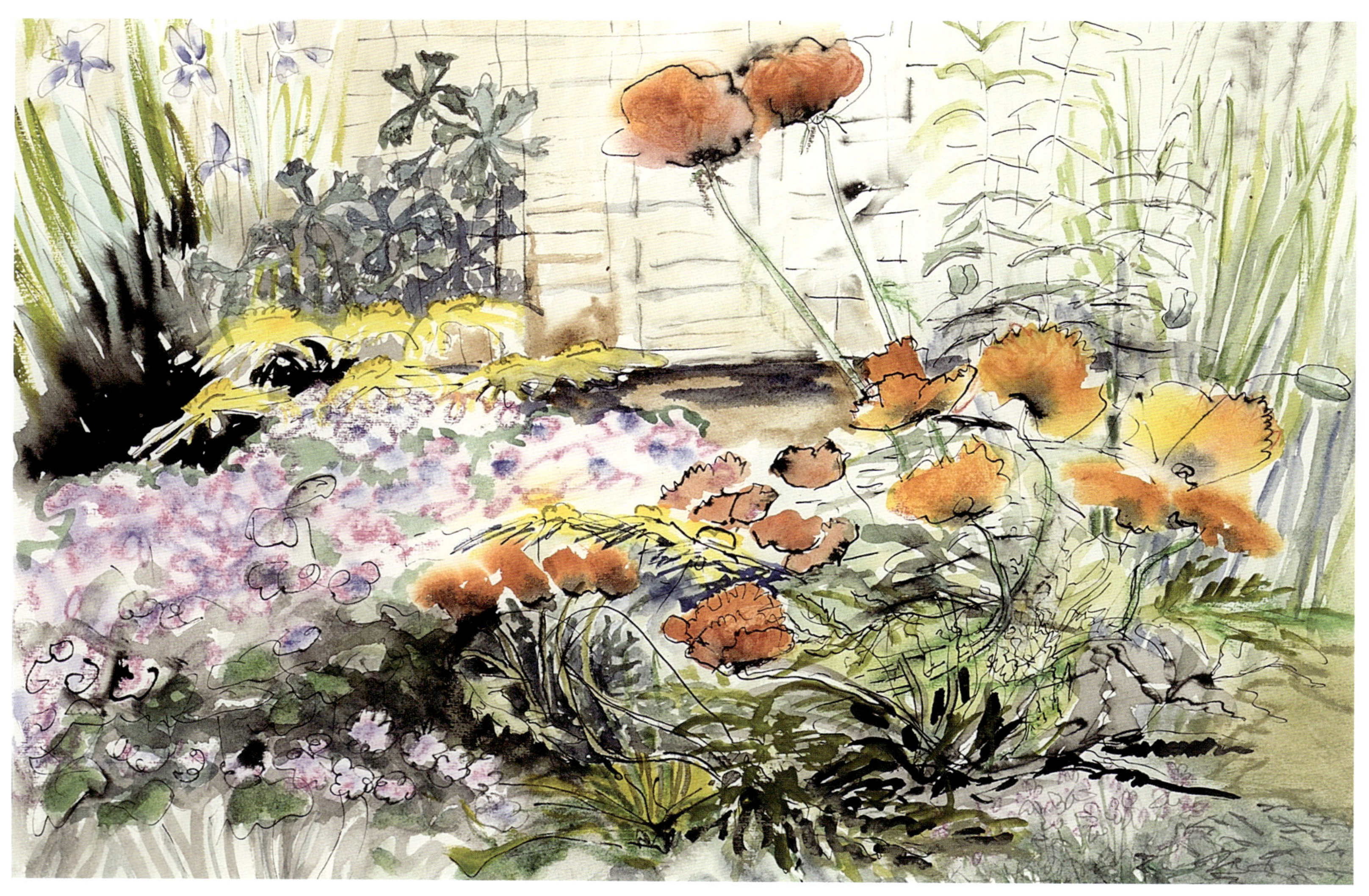

watercolour and ink 310 x 460mm

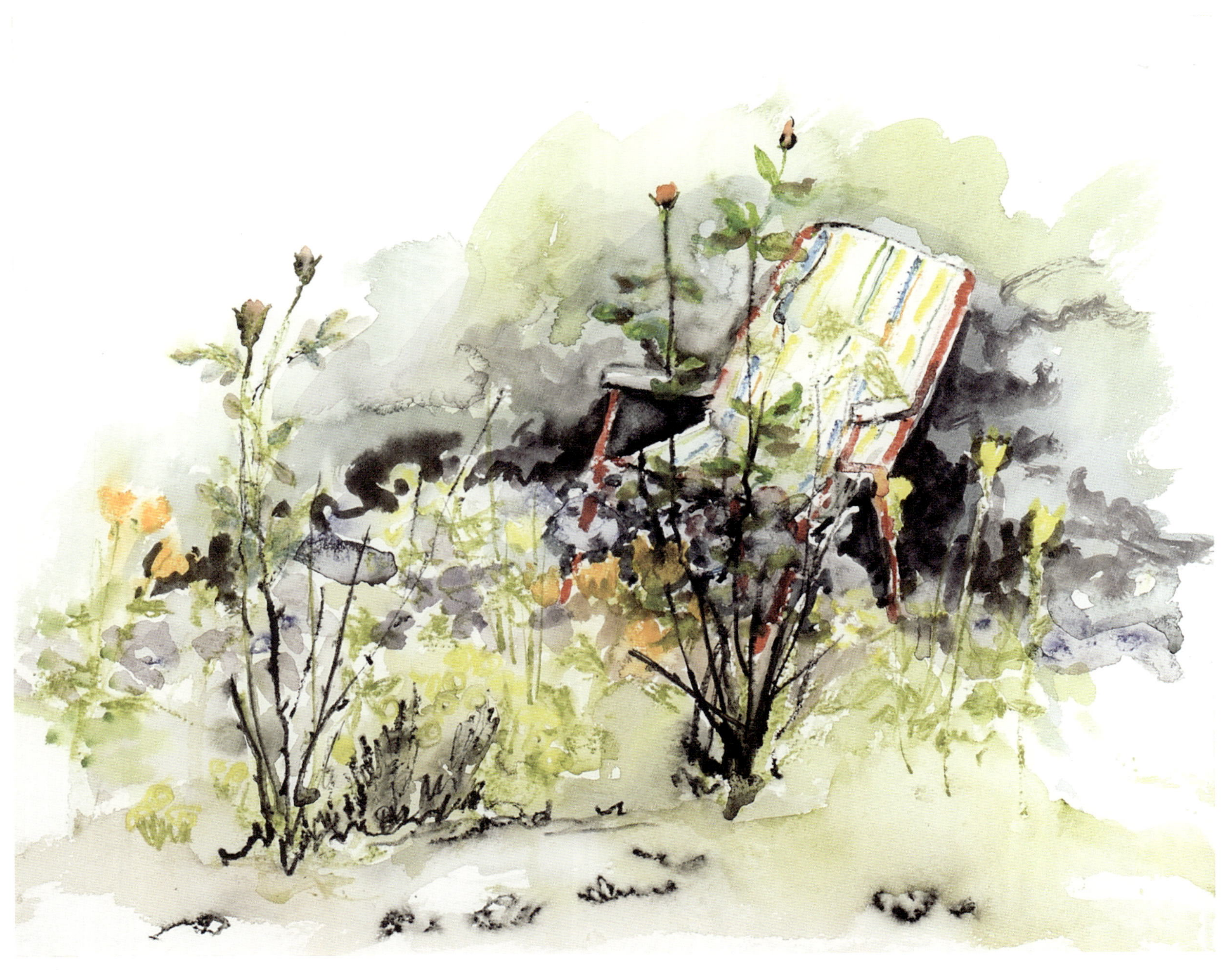

watercolour 291 x 375mm

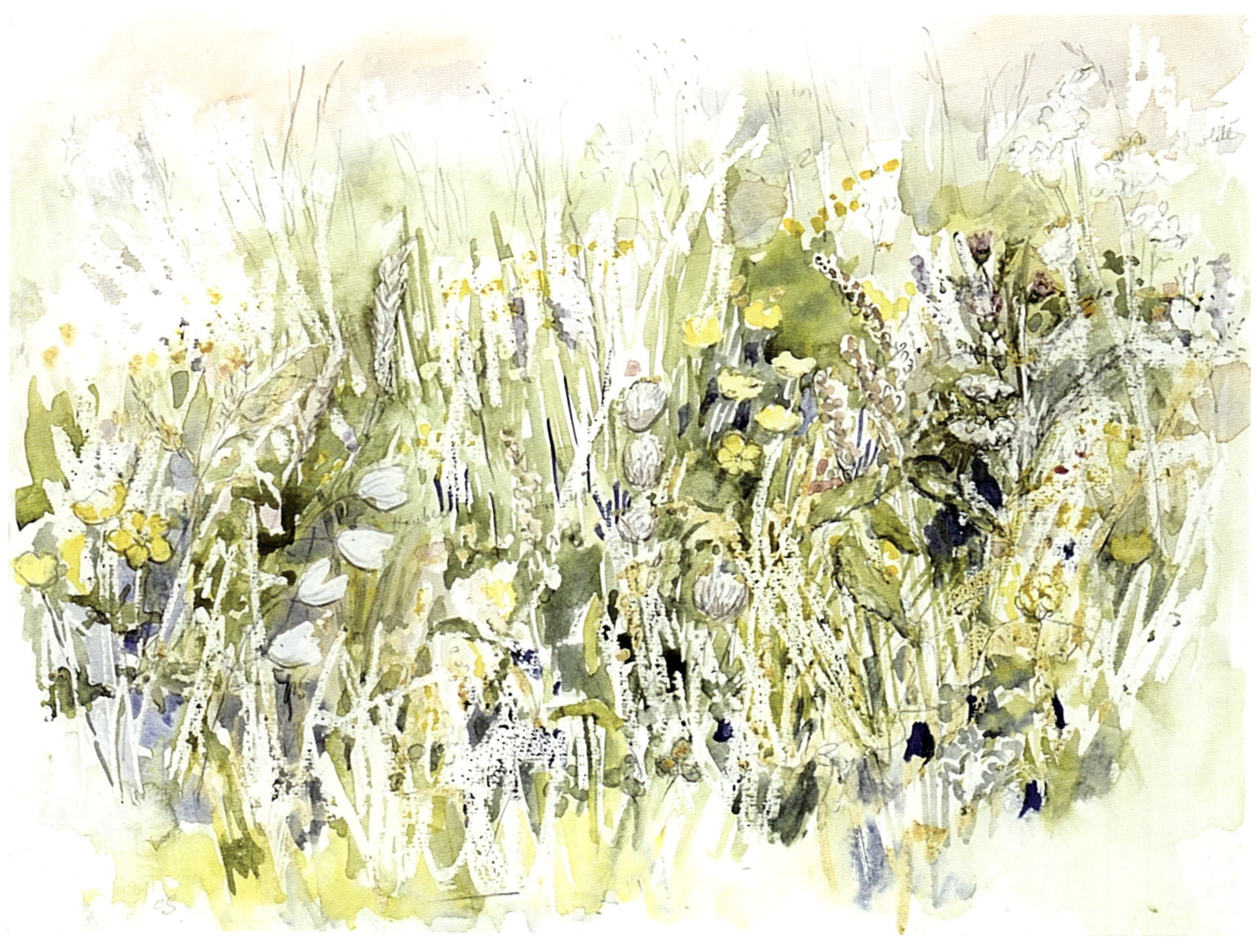

watercolour (on wax) 250 x 340mm

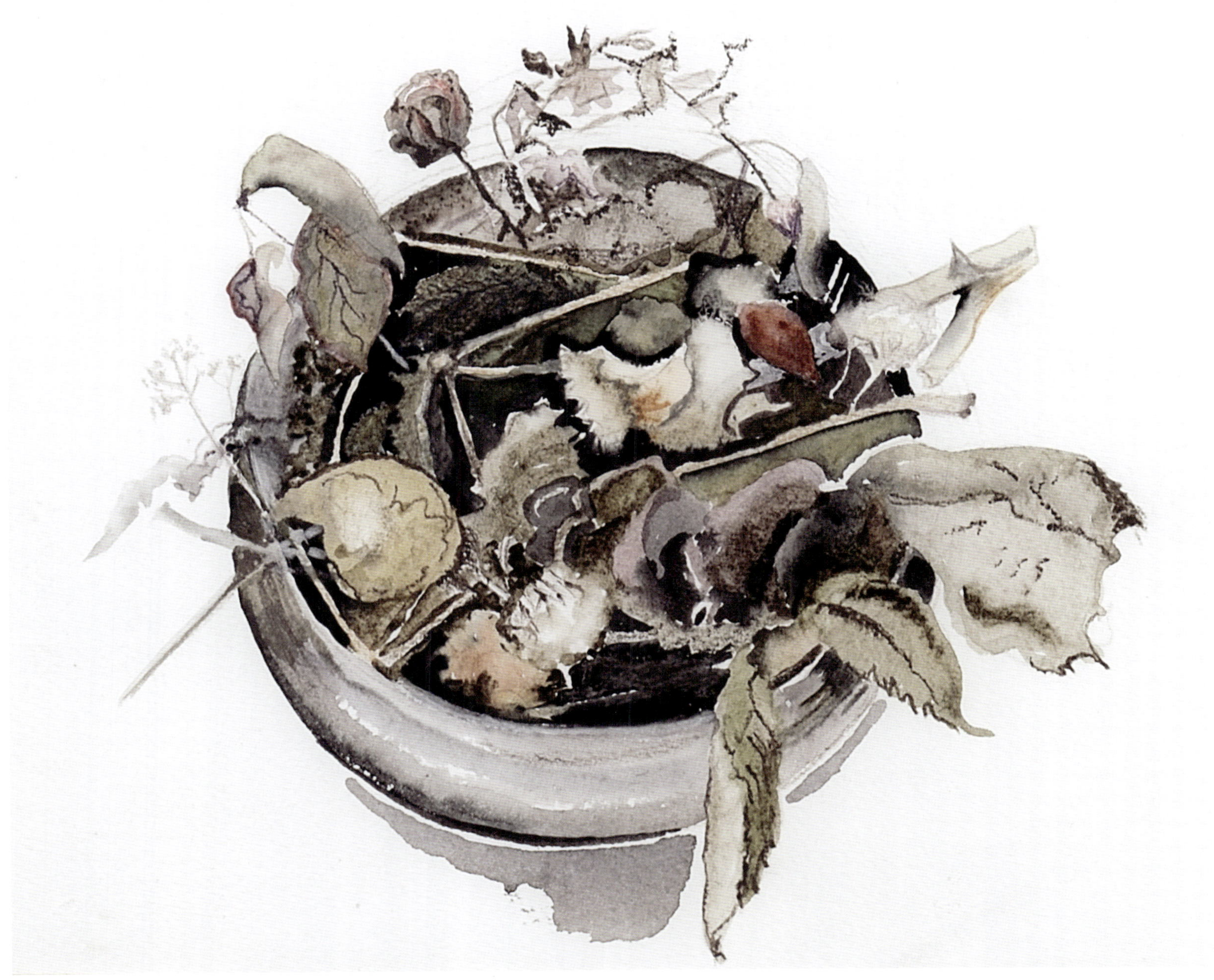

watercolour 200 x 255mm

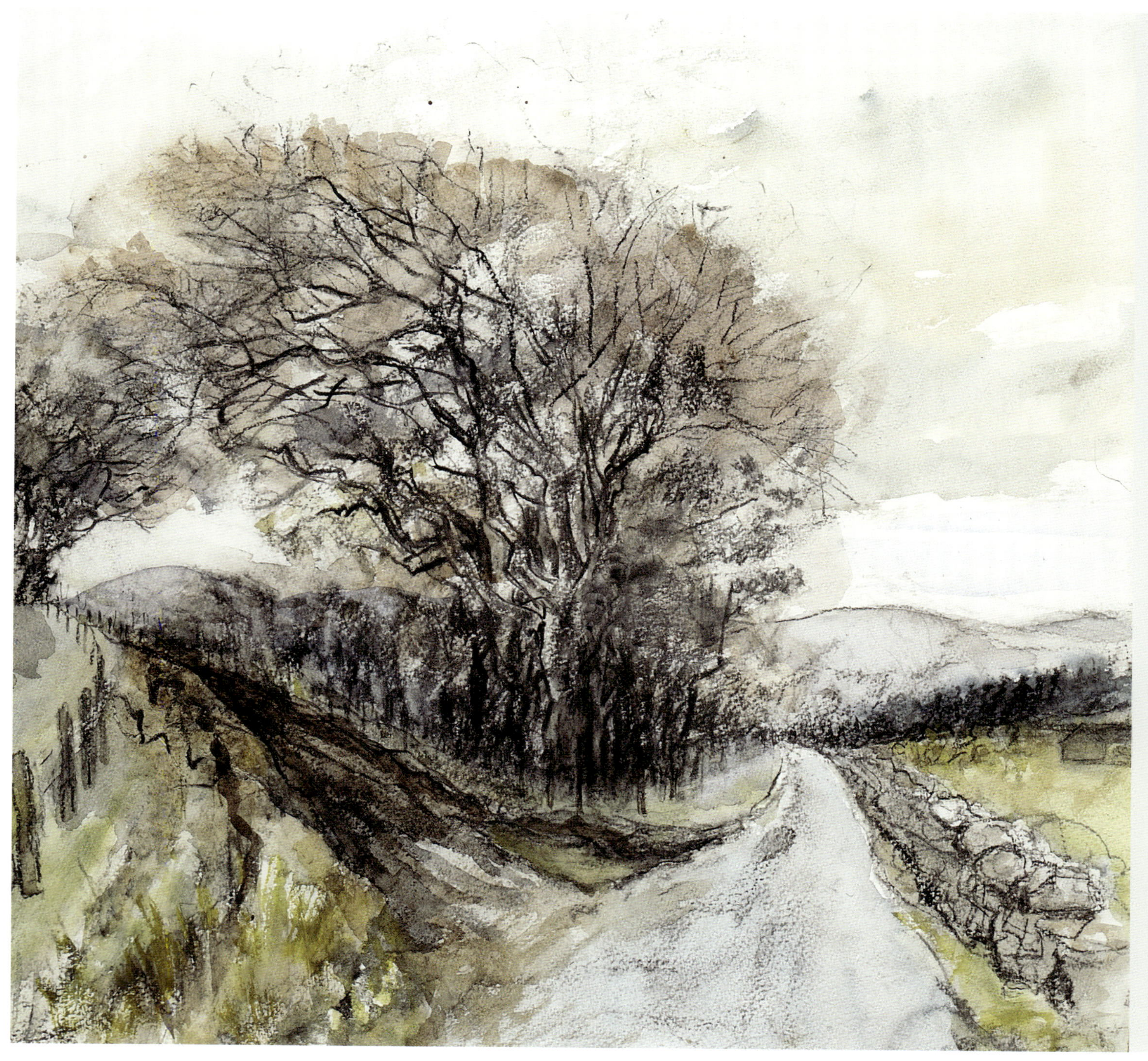

watercolour, charcoal and ink 380 x 480mm

The Track Divides

Homeward bound from Stonypath,
comes the point where a choice
must be made – which way to go?
I know them both. Will mood follow one,
or time dictate I take the other?
Or weather? More shelter to the left,
under arching trees; more daylight
to the right where Mendick Hill slopes
its shoulder down an open sky,
and further on, a welcome rest
awaits at the low wall of the bridge
in Lynedale's genteel hollow.

But today I take the faster track,
though darker, let it sweep me up:
too many questions crowd my mind
like the mud churning underfoot;
fence posts march on either side;
I count them with my stride –
they hold me in.

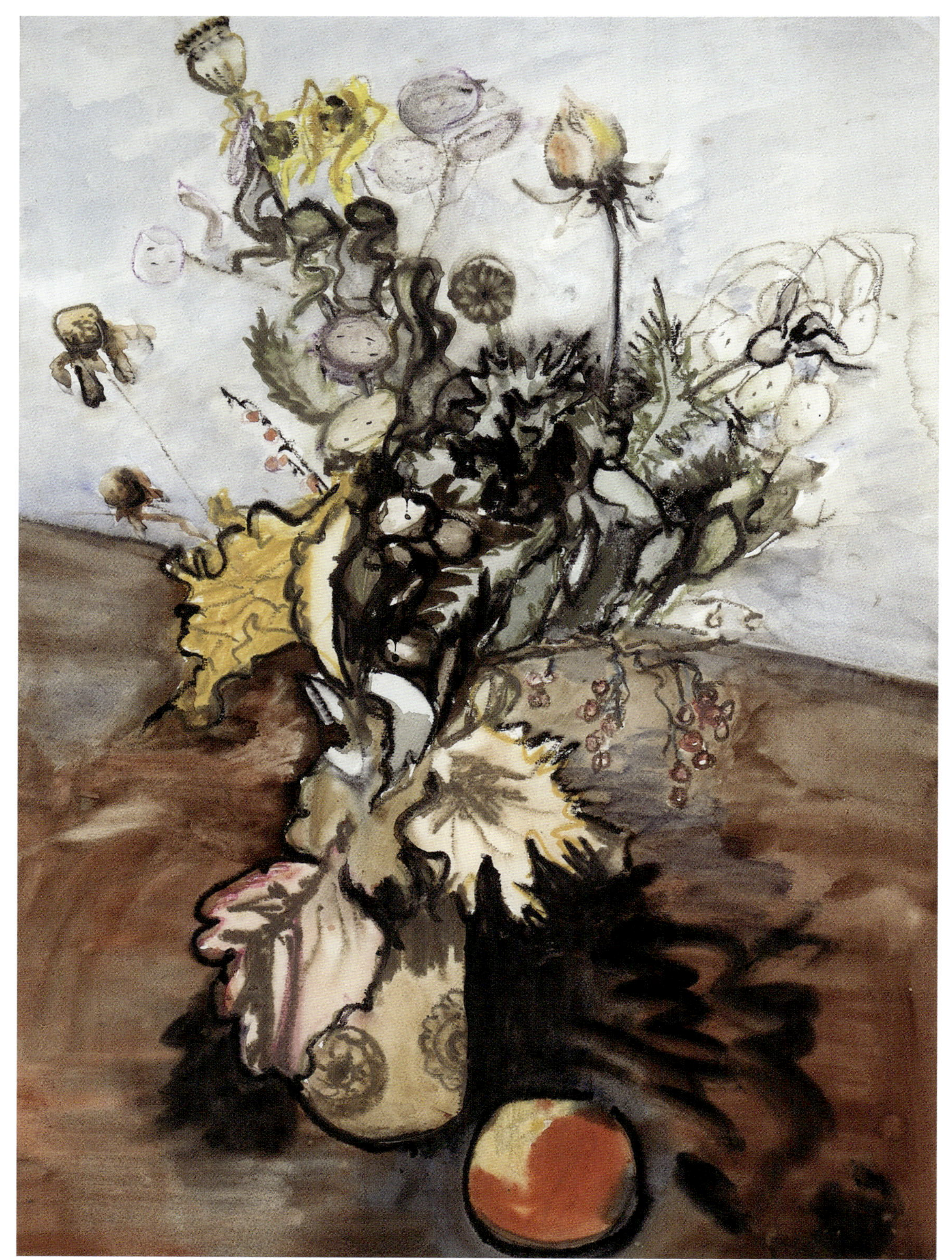

(left) watercolour 584 x 438mm
(opposite) watercolour and
charcoal 330 x 356mm

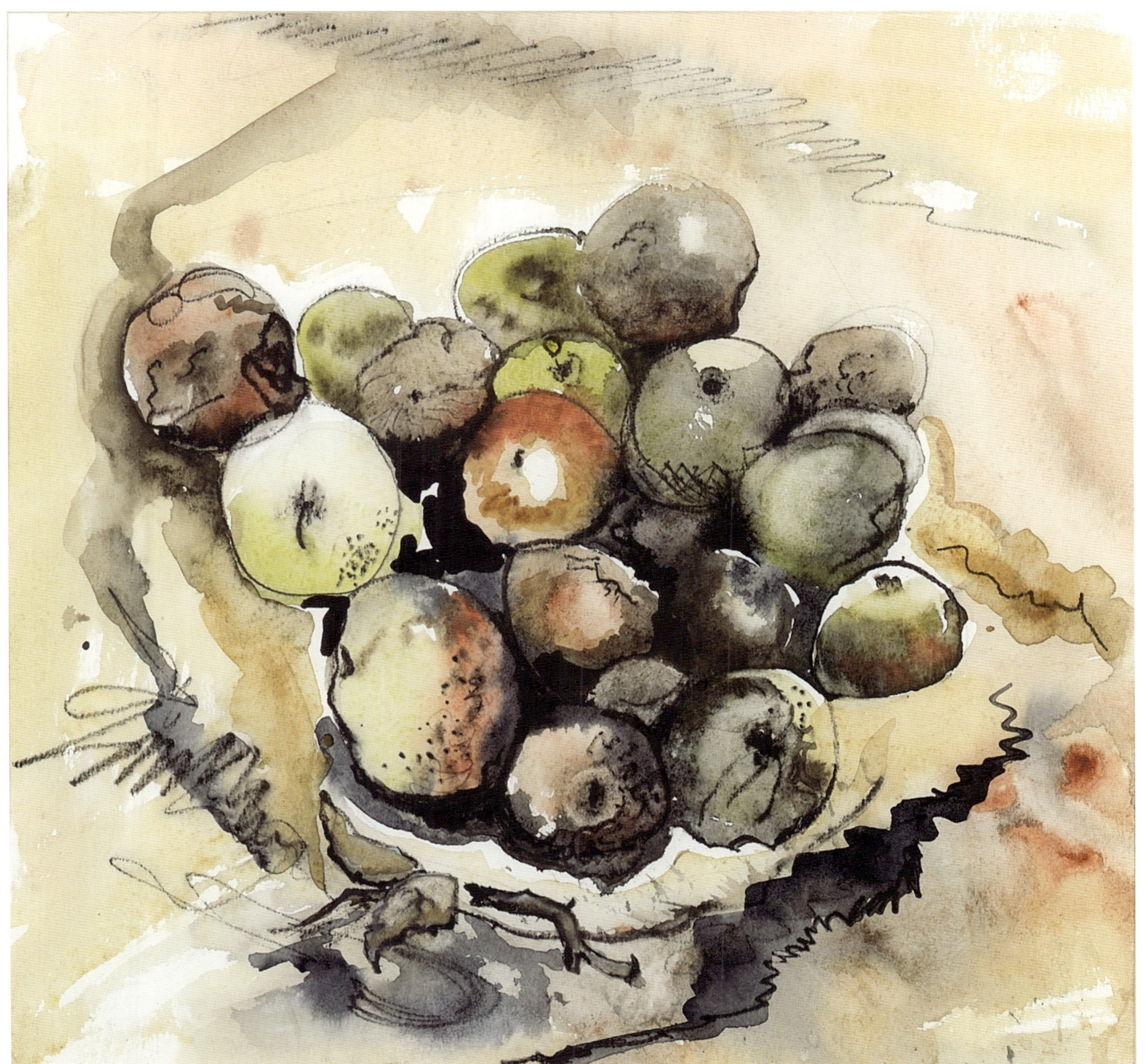

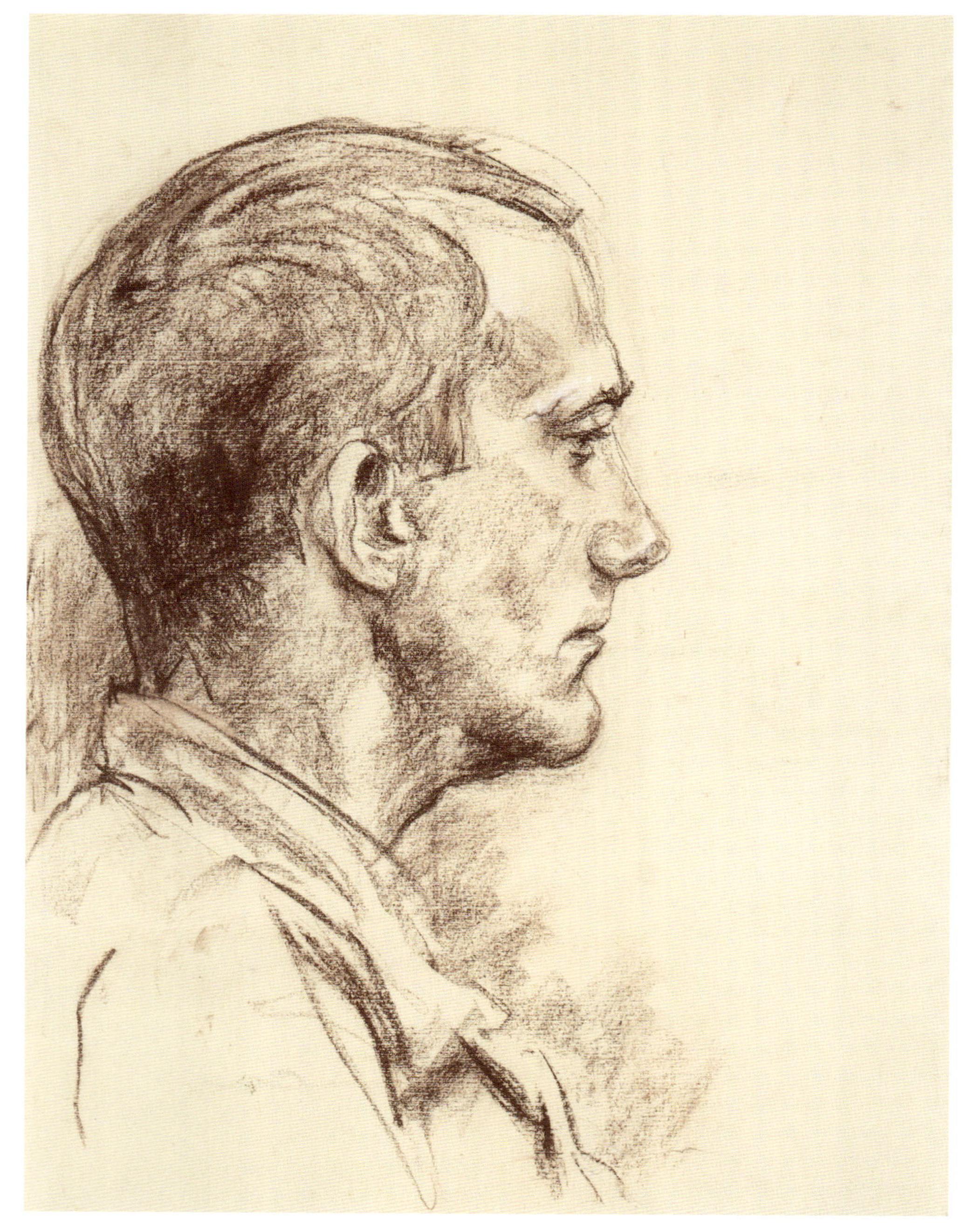

chalk 440 x 320mm

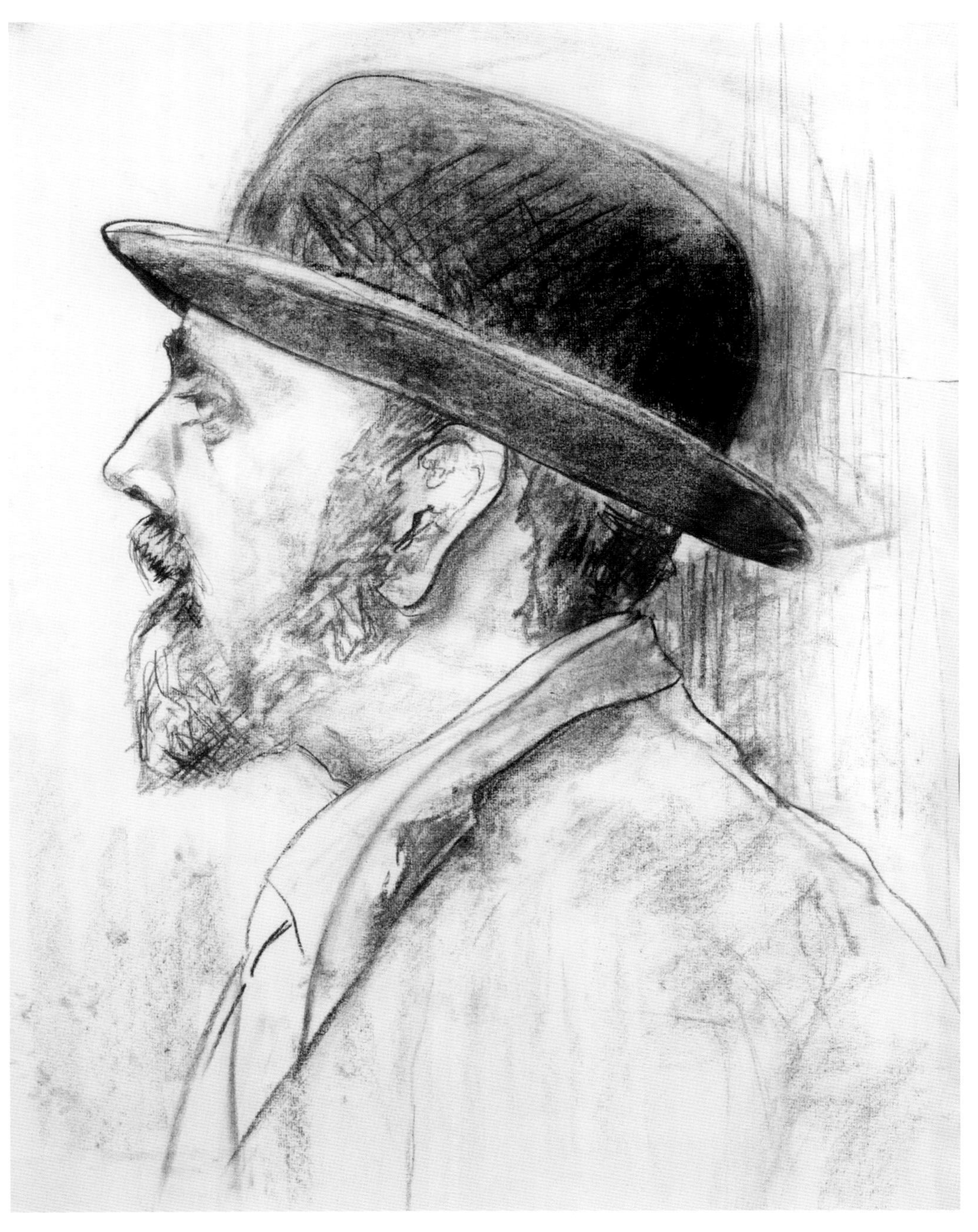

charcoal 700 x 500mm

Rose Stalks in Snow

My lines mark absence,
the long lack, when sap lies low
and only thorns show;

footprints my presence,
recorded ephemera
on yesterday's snow.

White fills in blank space,
telling tales of buried things;
silence – no bird sings.

Hoarfrost-wizened leaves
cling to withered tendrils, chilled
remnants in stilled air.

At eyeline's corner,
edging my monochrome frame,
faded berries stain.

Though this season numbs,
I'll bide my time till Spring's core
calls colour from the store.

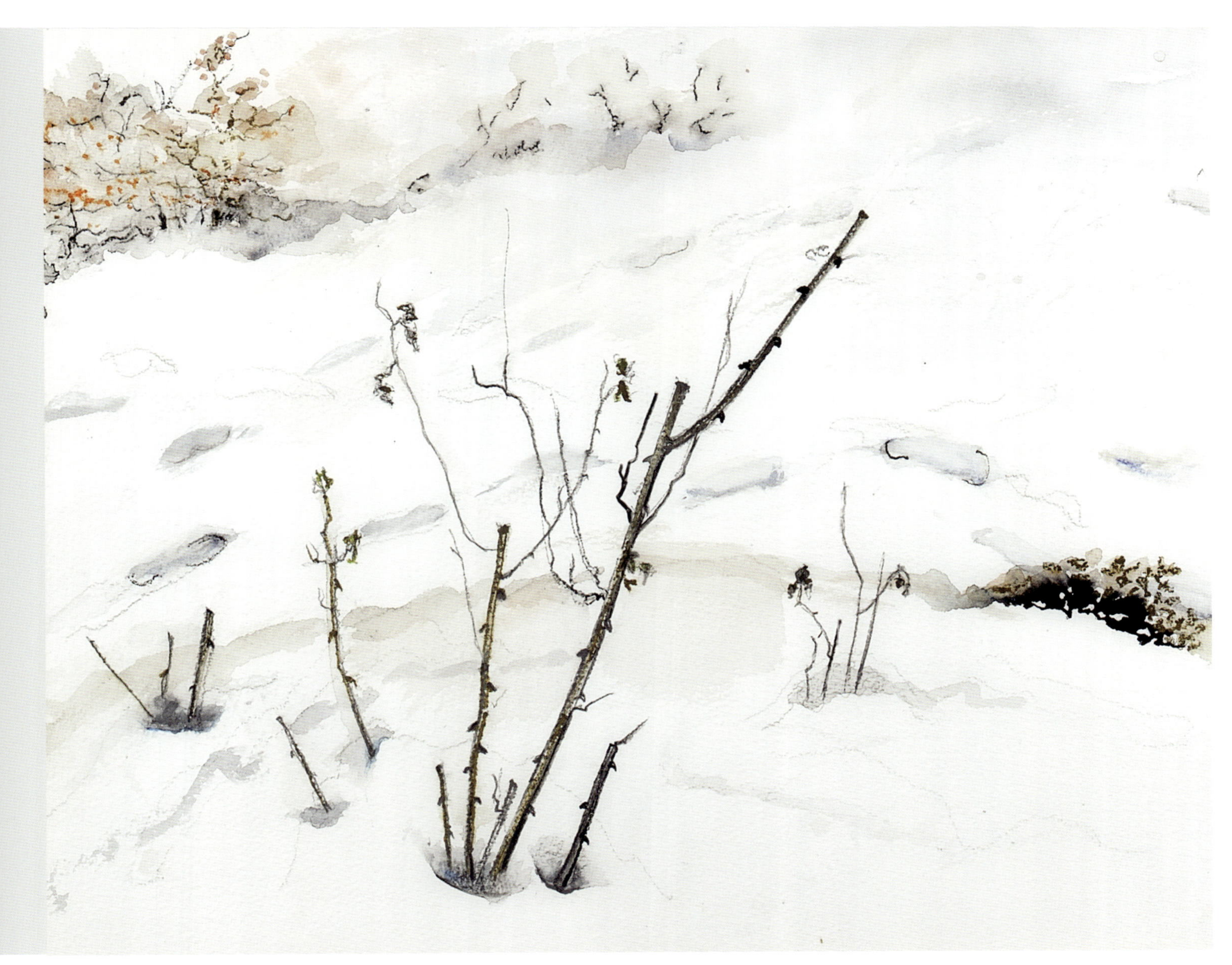

watercolour 290 x 390mm

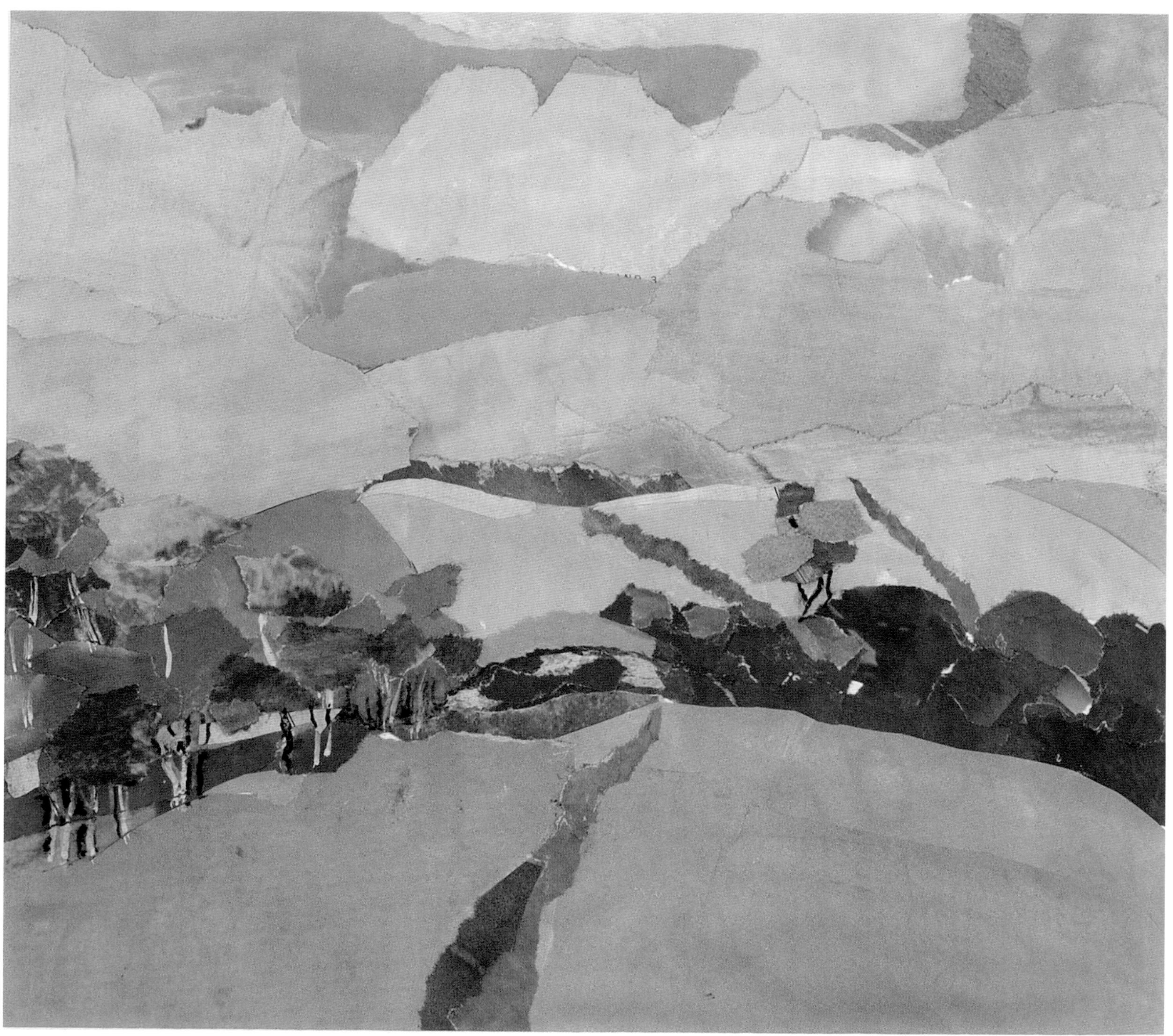

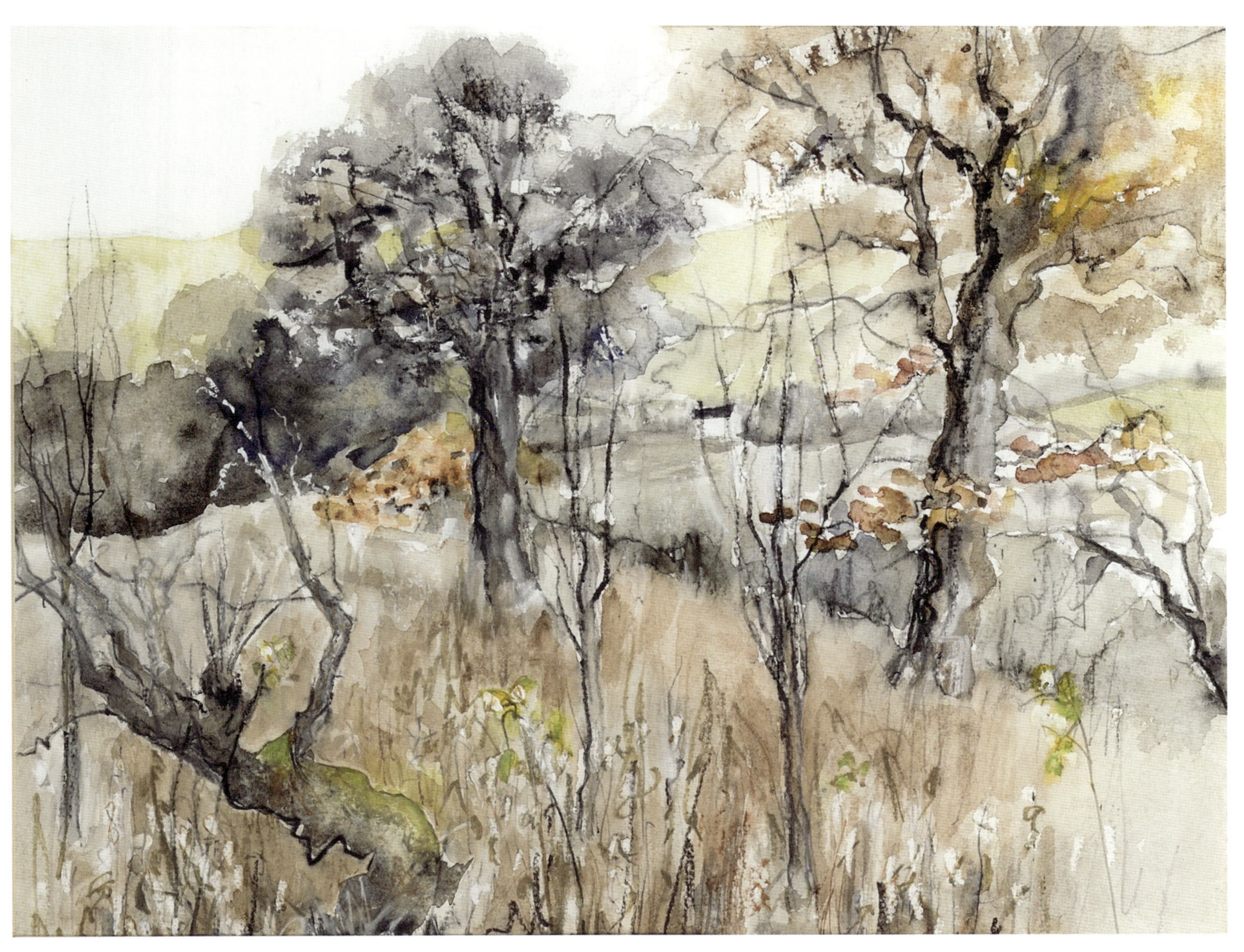

(above) watercolour 290 x 390mm

(opposite) paper collage and watercolour 279 x 321mm

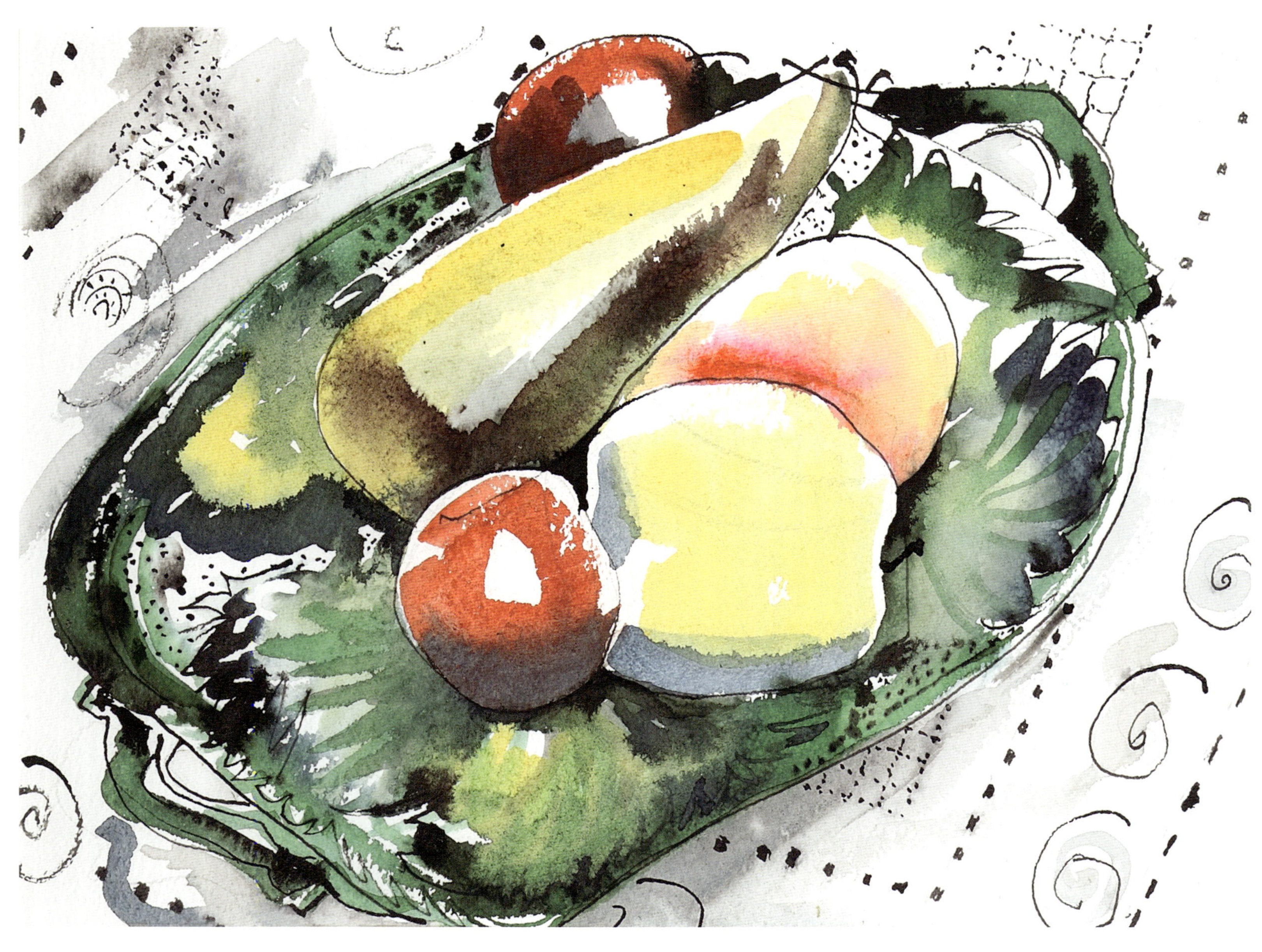

watercolour and ink 287 x 395mm

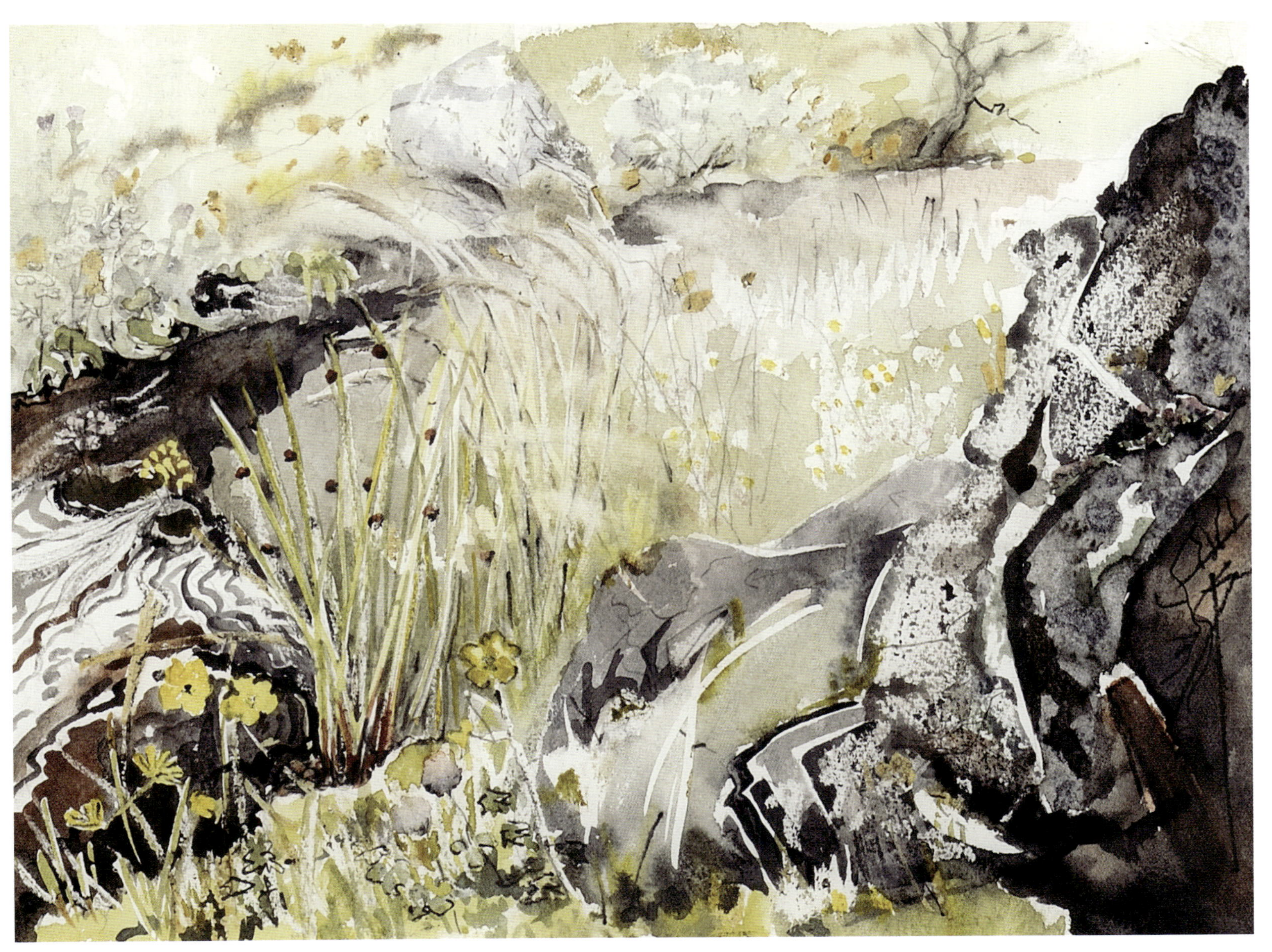

watercolour 248 x 338mm

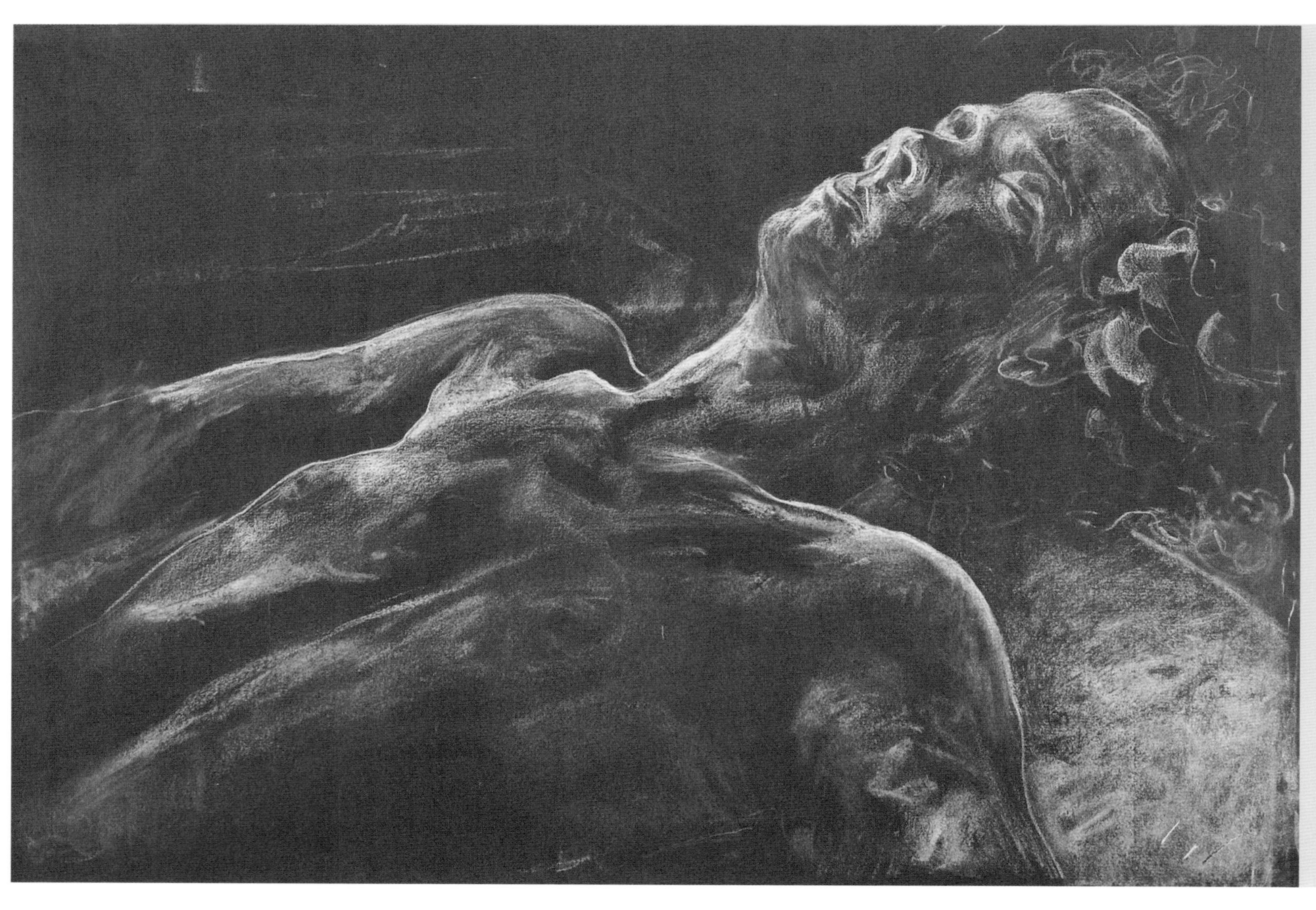

chalk 410 x 596mm

Sleeping Nude

You've slipped into the underworld,
a vault hollowed from brown peat;
snow has blown on the wind's tail
down a hidden tunnel to this cool lair –
deep as your sleep – dusting your contours
and the cold stone pillow beneath your head,
as if to preserve a narcotic state,
a limbo of welcome release.

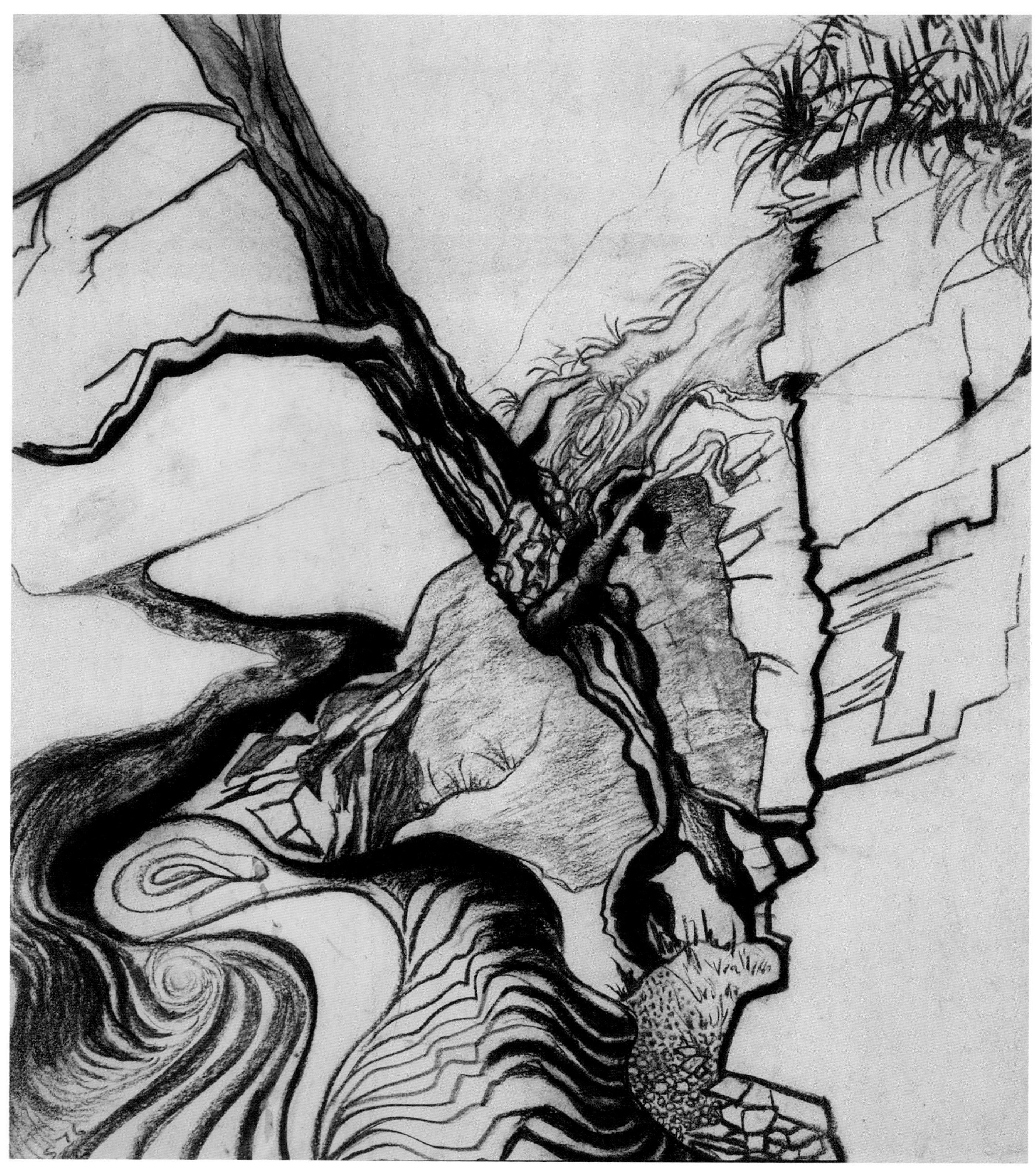

charcoal and ink

560 x 520mm

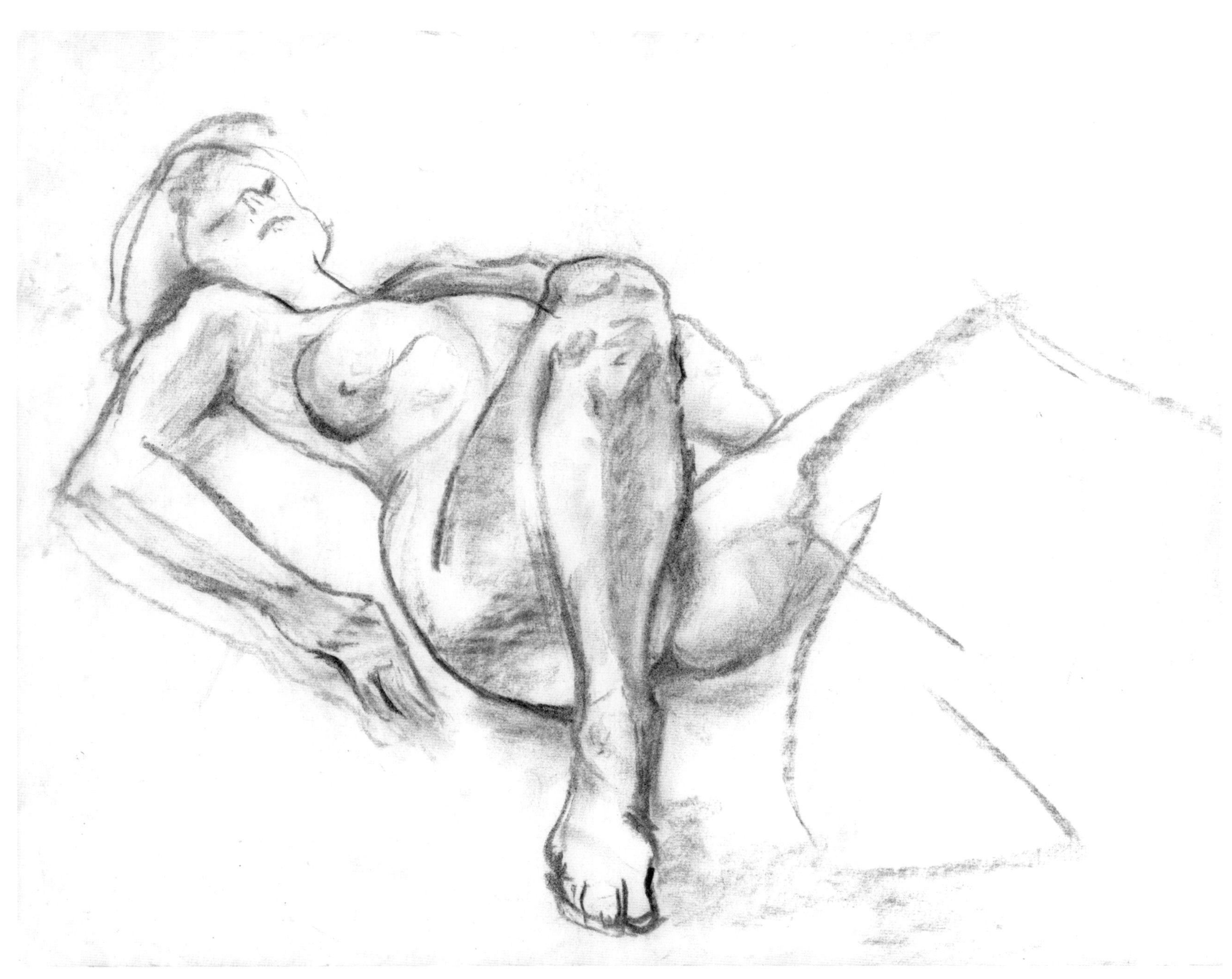

charcoal 297 x 420mm

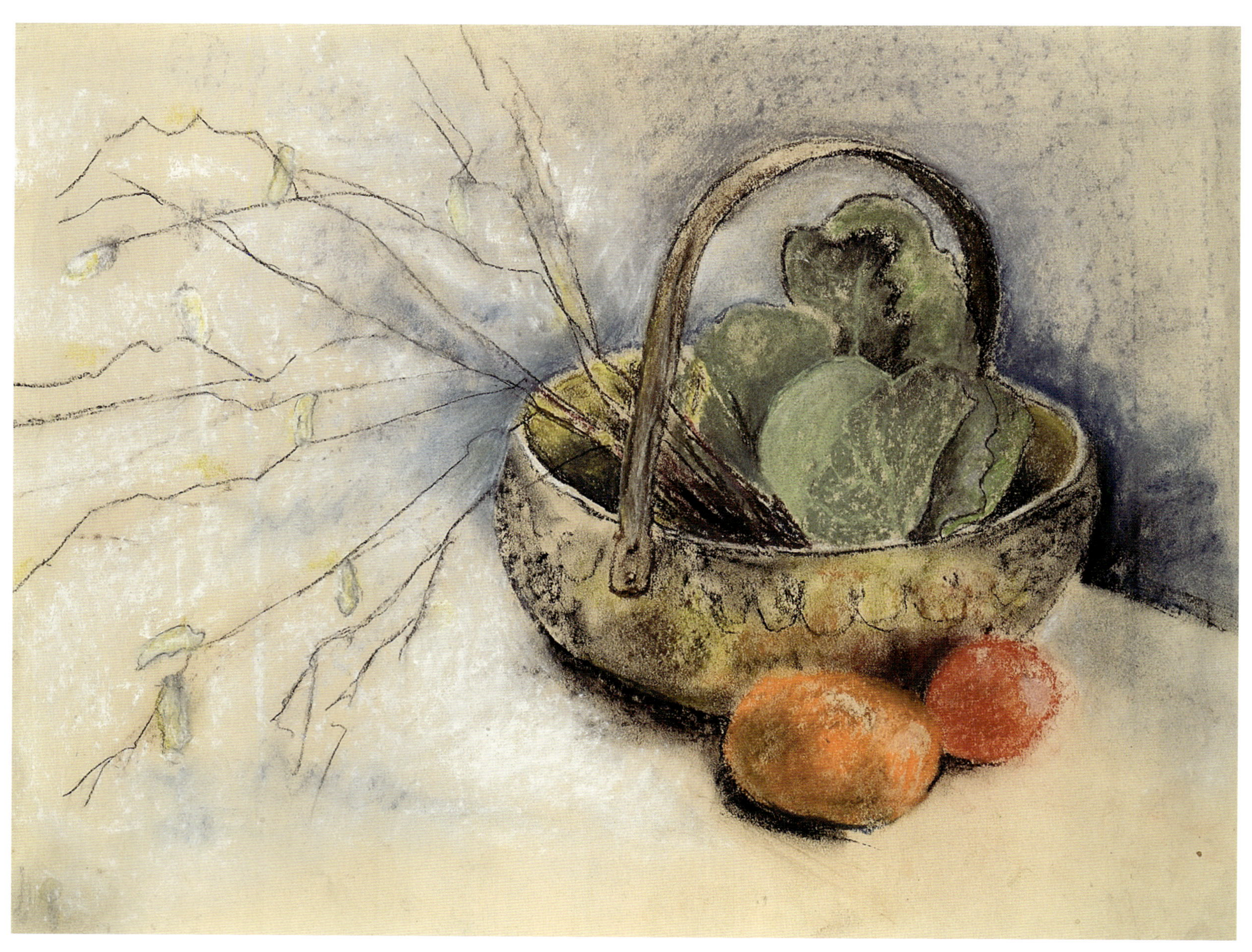

chalk 415 x 575mm

*"A chair. One of a pair. I have the
female half left behind after the
divorce. The larger one, the male,
has gone to a house unknown to
me. This chair hides behind the
kitchen door – a dropping place,
the transition between indoors
and outdoors. I hover between
the two when the sun emerges.
A knitted beret and scarf: small
amounts of wool, using up
leftovers from a grander project;
a blue jacket faced with orange.
Opposite where I sit, always in my
line of vision, the chair waits for
a knock at the door and a chance
hour of company to talk about
books, village news and world
events."*

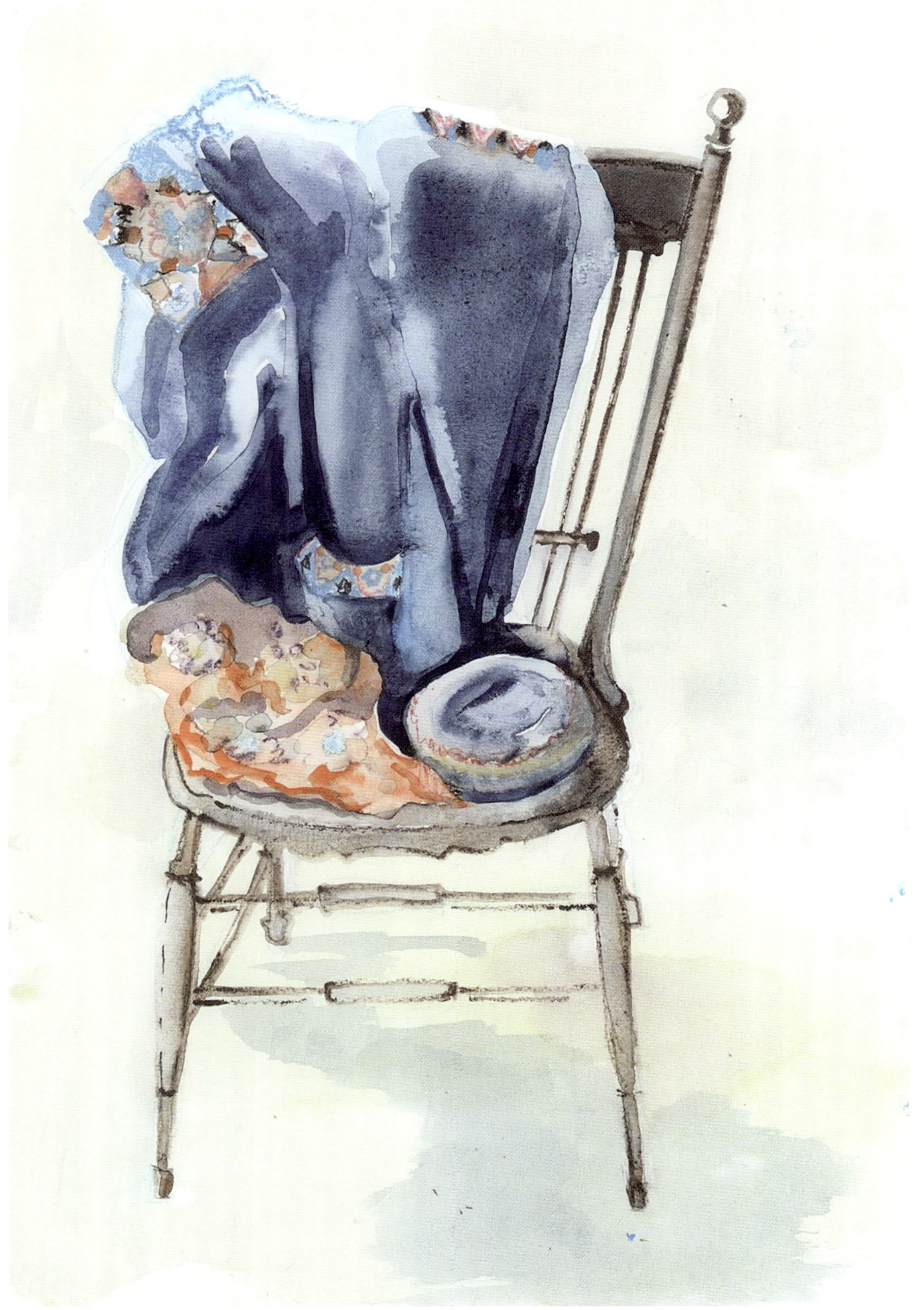

watercolour 412 x 212mm

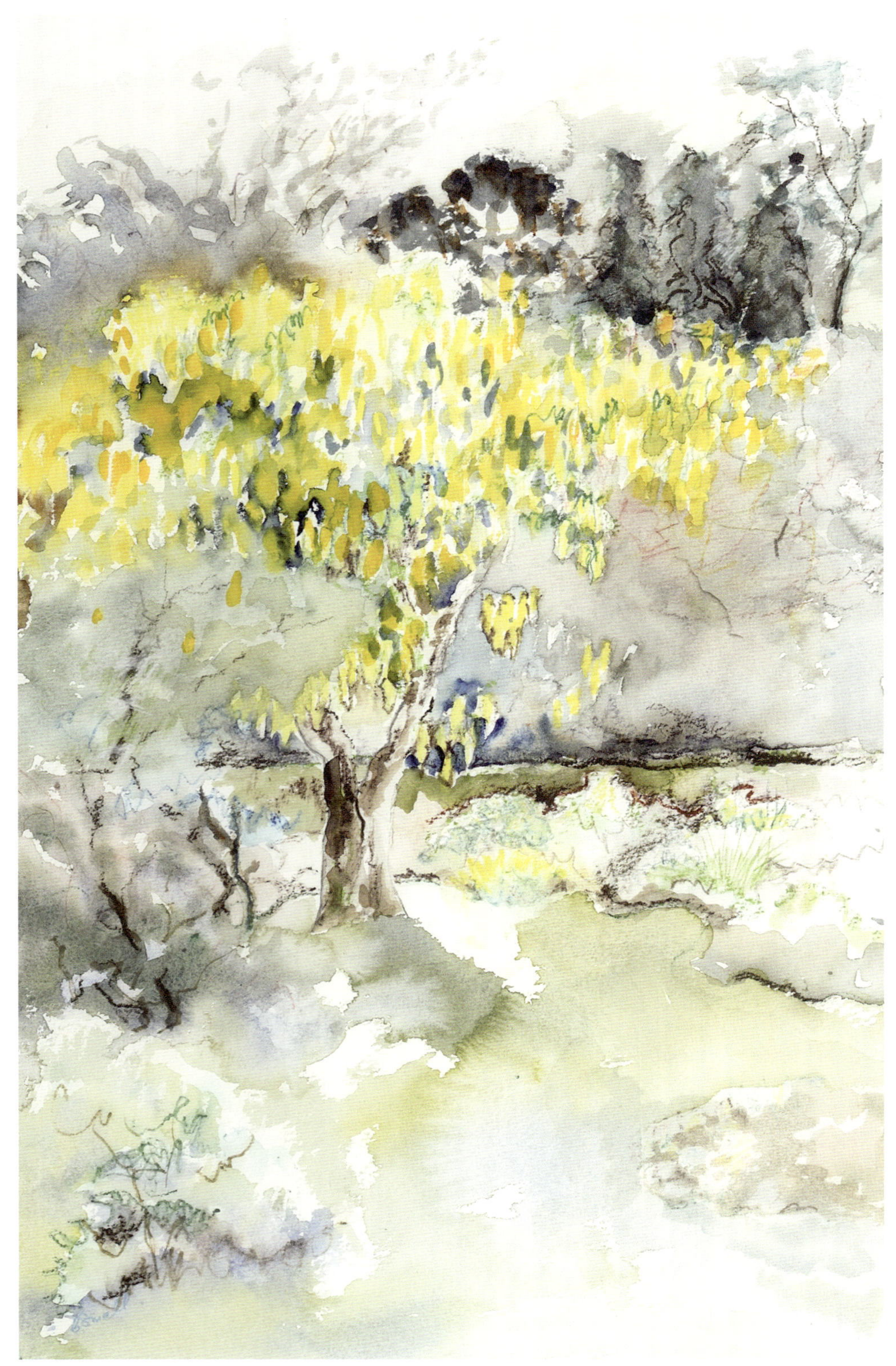

watercolour and charcoal 550 x 360mm

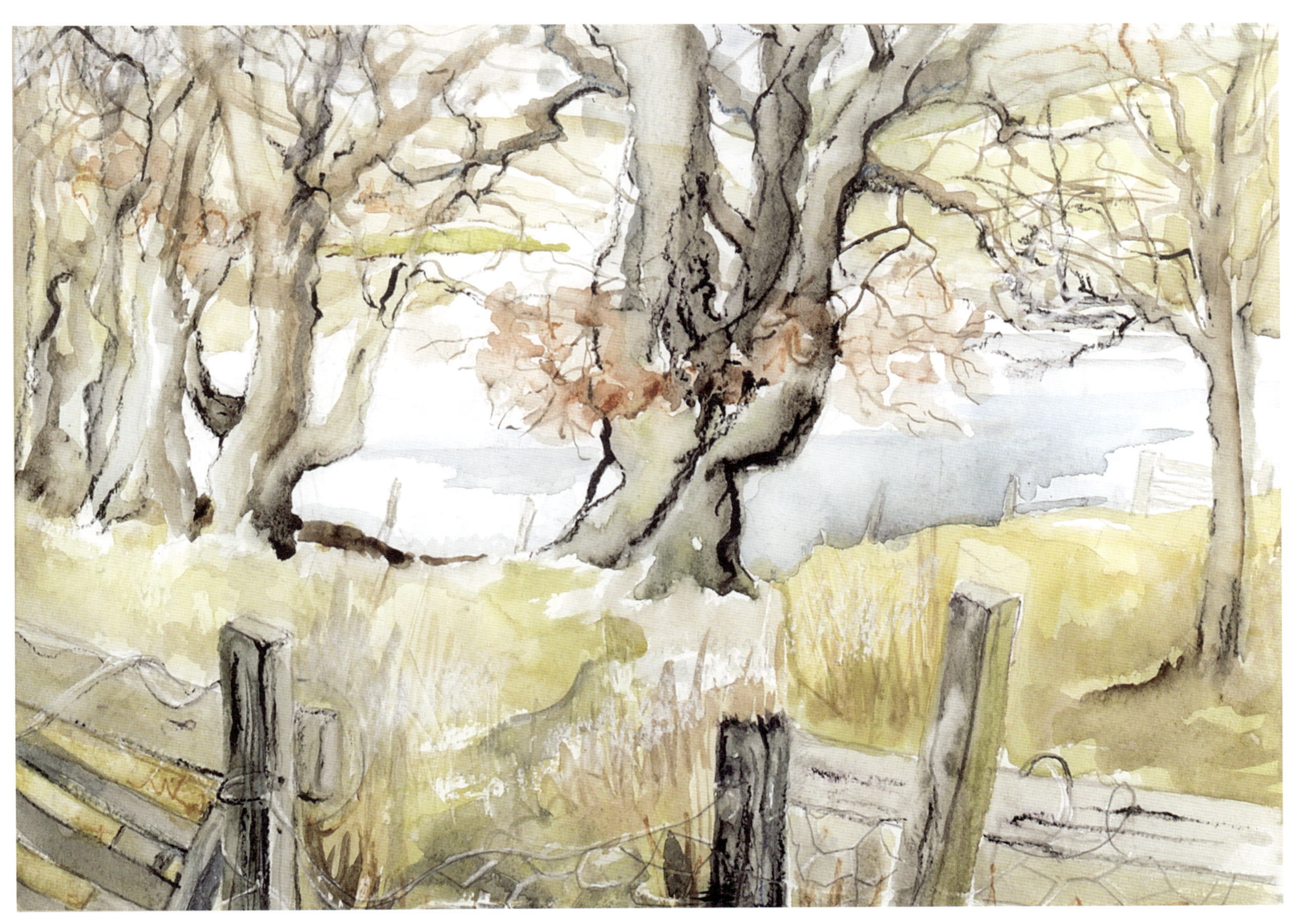

watercolour 250 x 358mm

Tea for Two

Your battered lid only adds
to your appeal – we adapt
to each other's ageing grip,
the decades' wear and tear;
there's comfort in the way
you offer familiar resistance,
and in your ritual release
of scented loose-leaf, always scooped
with the same engraved silver spoon;
your faded floral décor never fails
to delight; we are the original tea for two,
and two for tea, you and me.

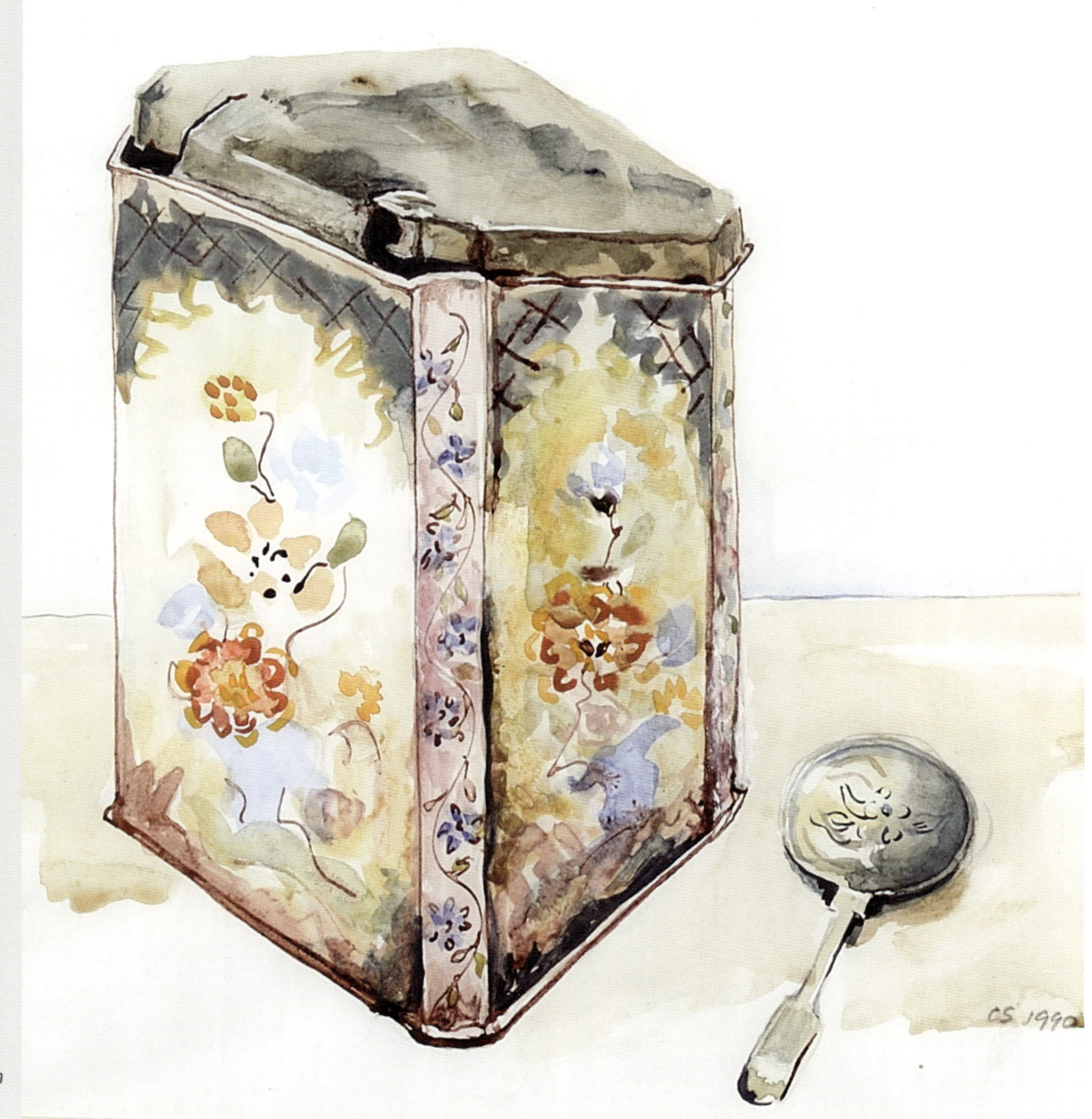

watercolour 280 x 240mm

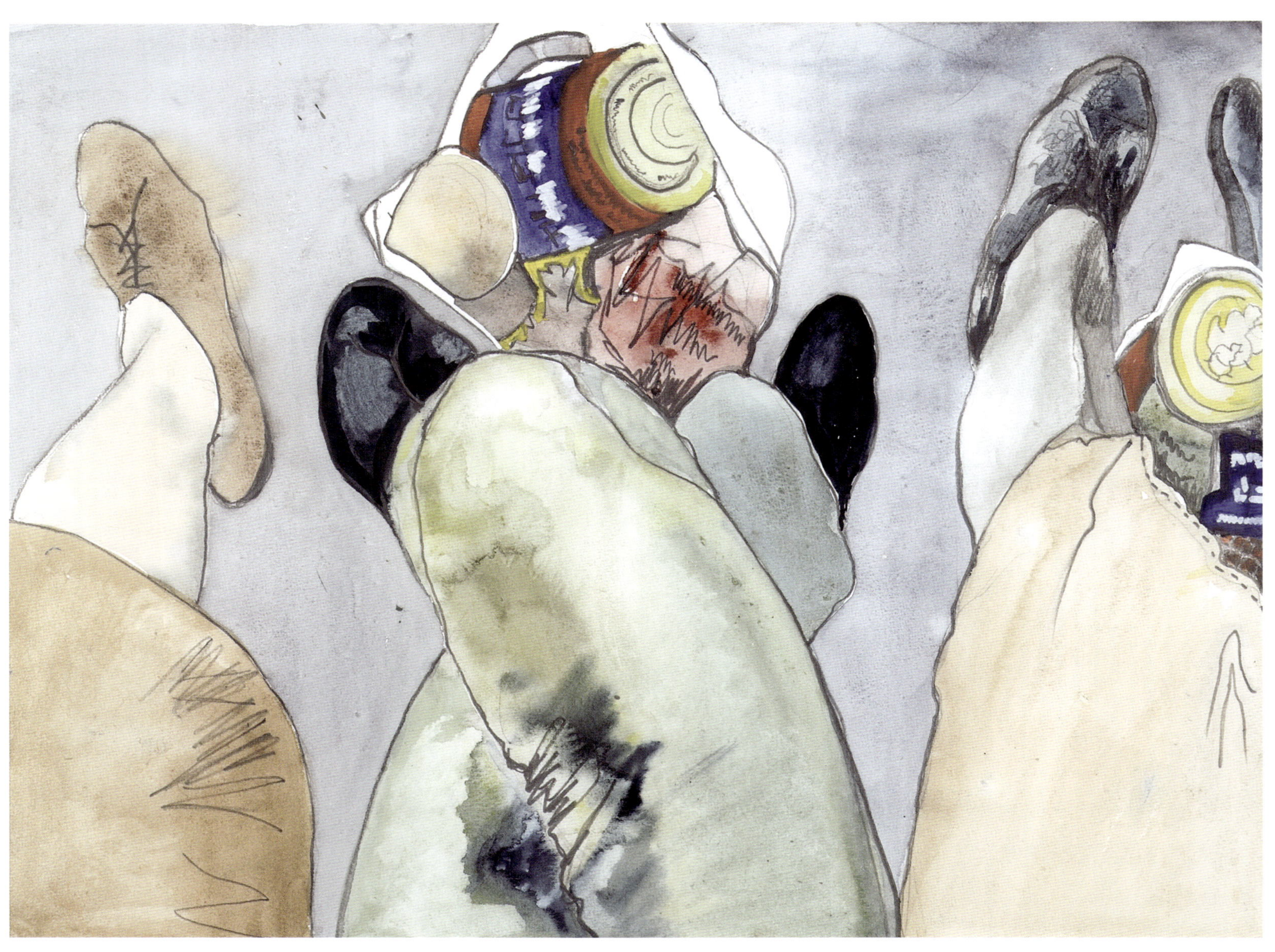

watercolour 353 x 488mm

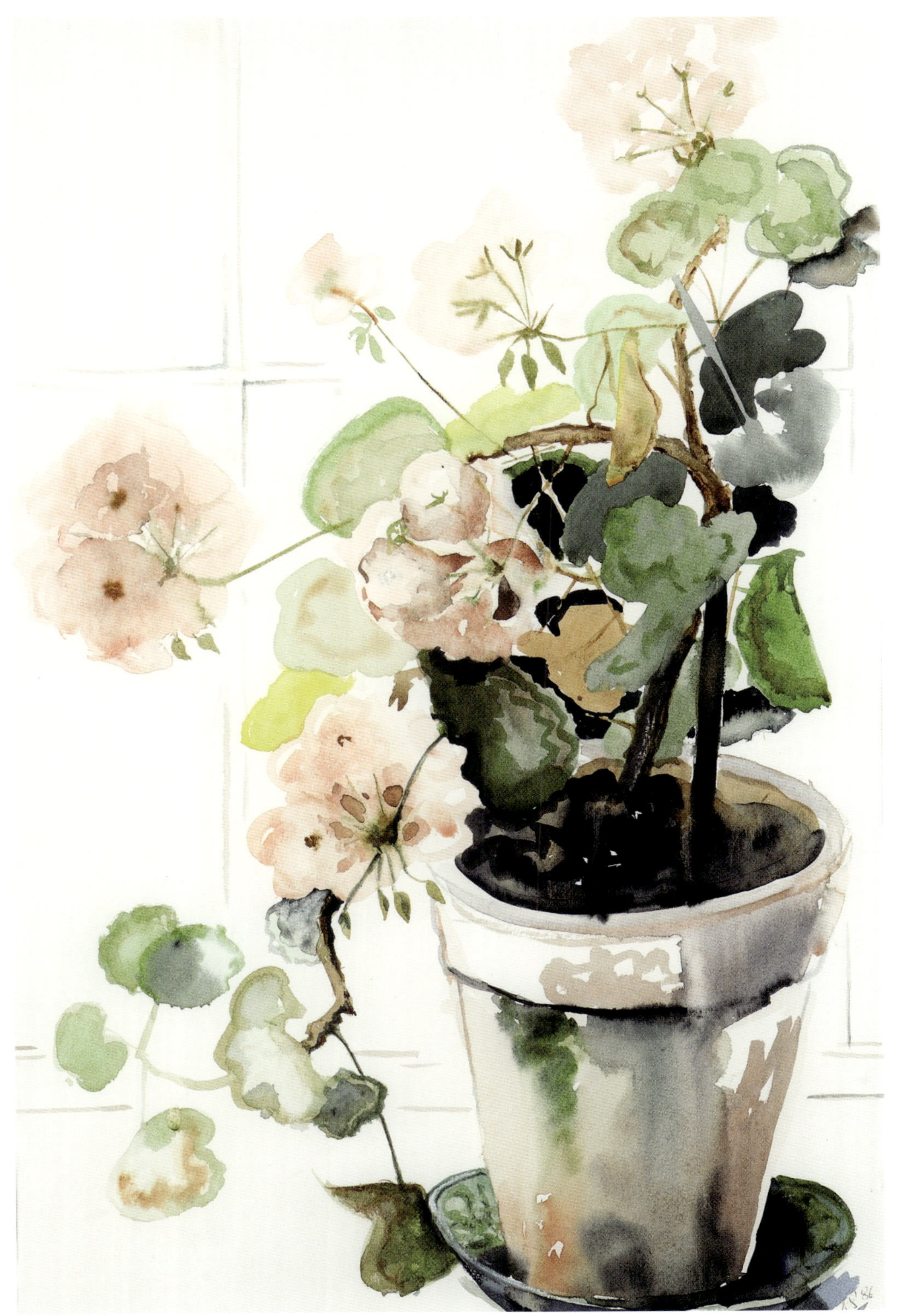

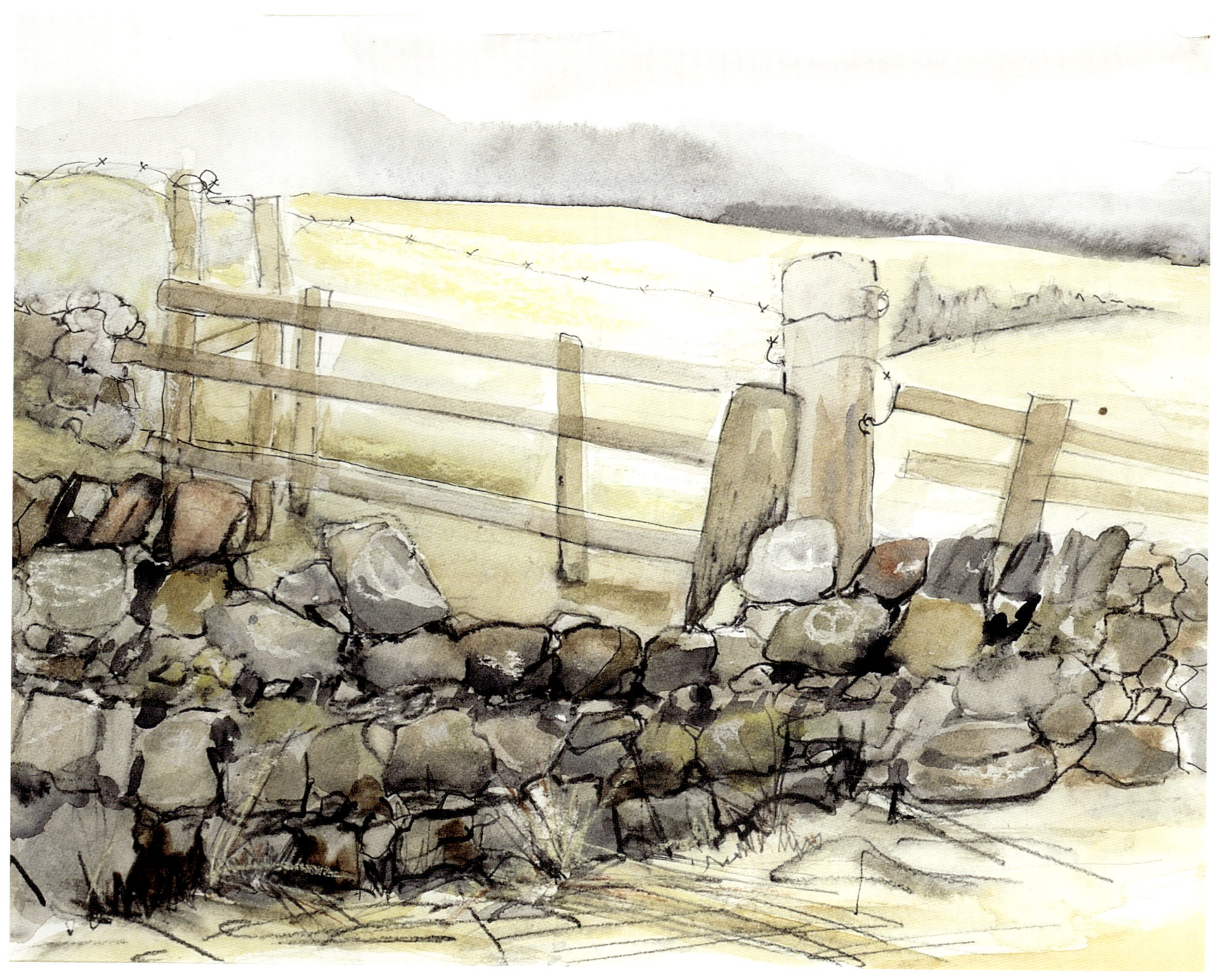

watercolour and ink 250 x 320mm

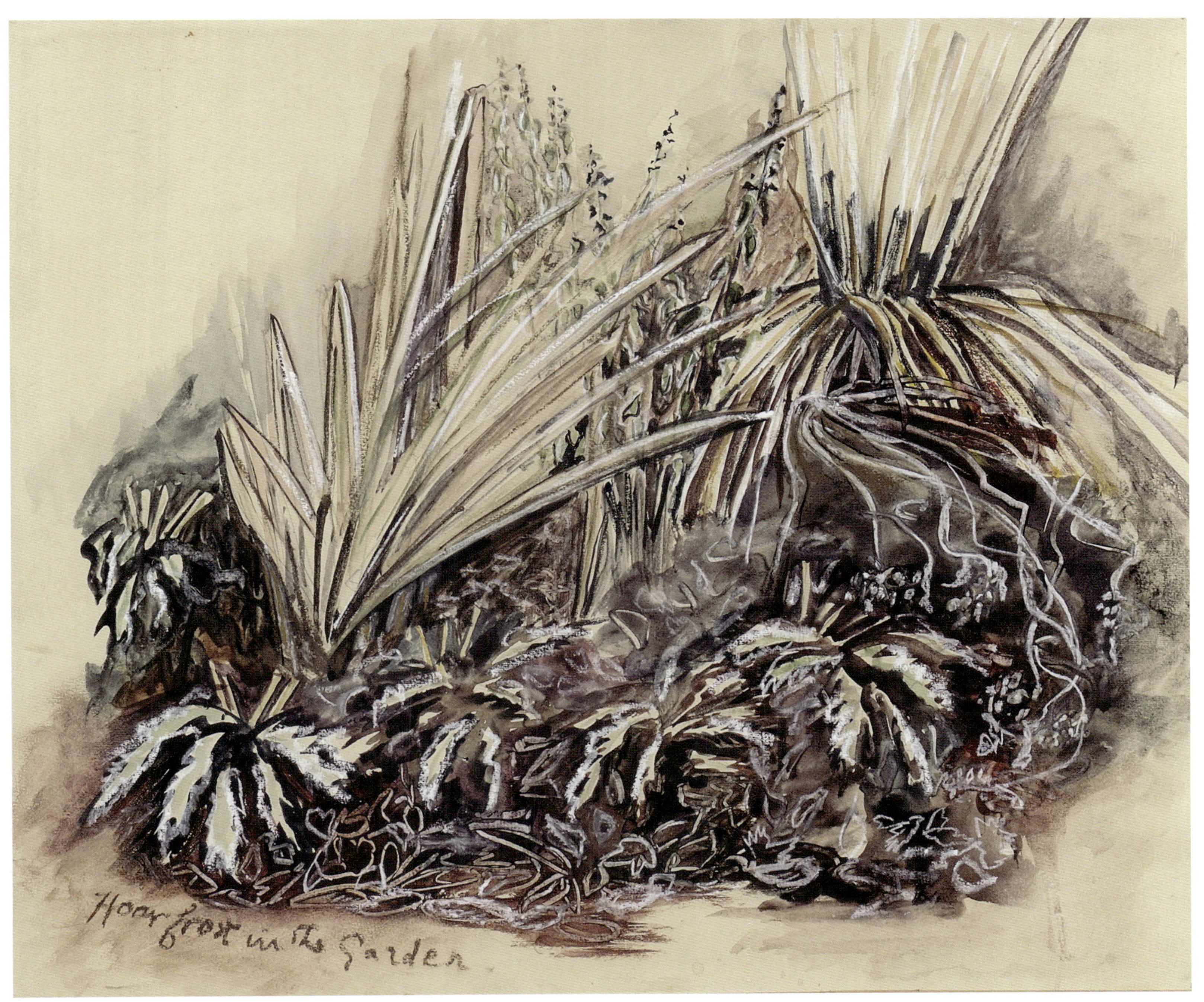

watercolour and chalk 370 x 460mm

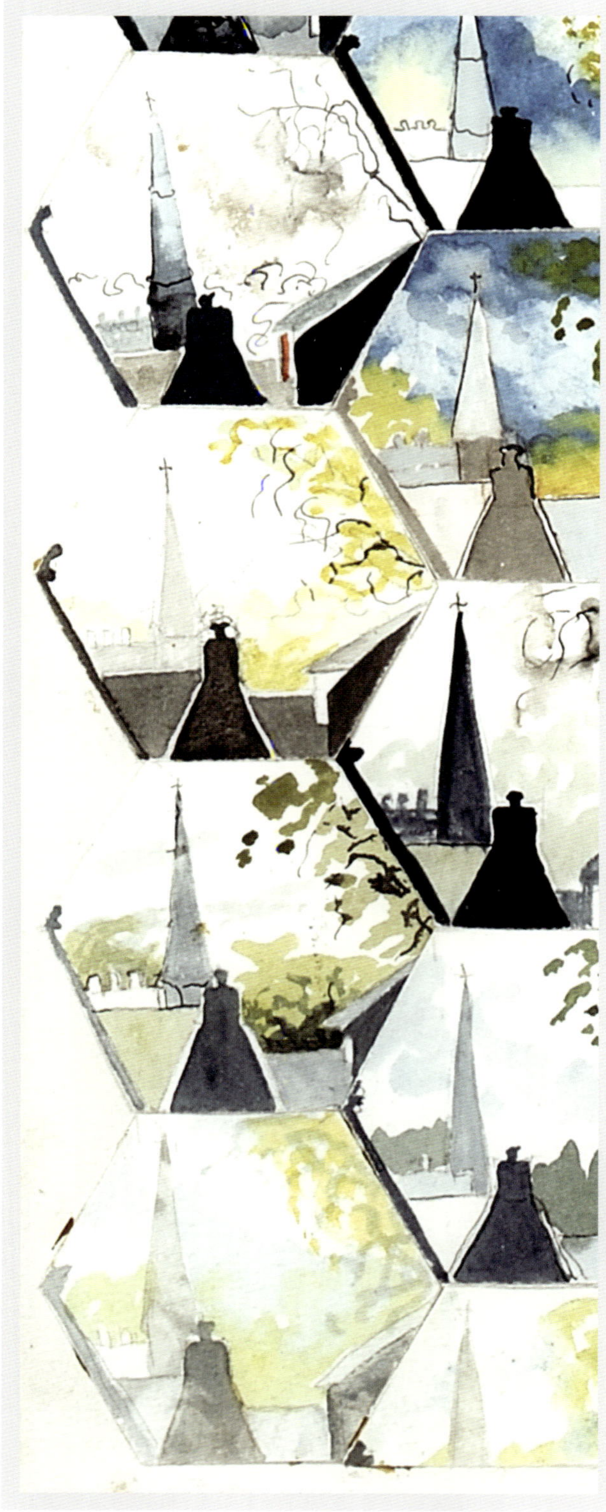

Eighty Days from a Single Frame

My world has narrowed with age,
my field of vision tighter now –
I focus on fewer things, but closer;
the view from my window
never stays the same – every day
a variation, a modulation held
within a fixed, familiar frame:
a trinity of triangles – church spire,
chimney stack, a slice of pitched roof,
the prominence of each contingent
on the daily disposition of the sun;
branches spread and sway
their seasonal tracery across the sky
to mediate the space, until mist
seeps in, diluting stone, brick and bark
to mere ghosts – each stage
of saturation paler than the last –
and then dissolves the whole.

watercolour and ink 690 x 513mm

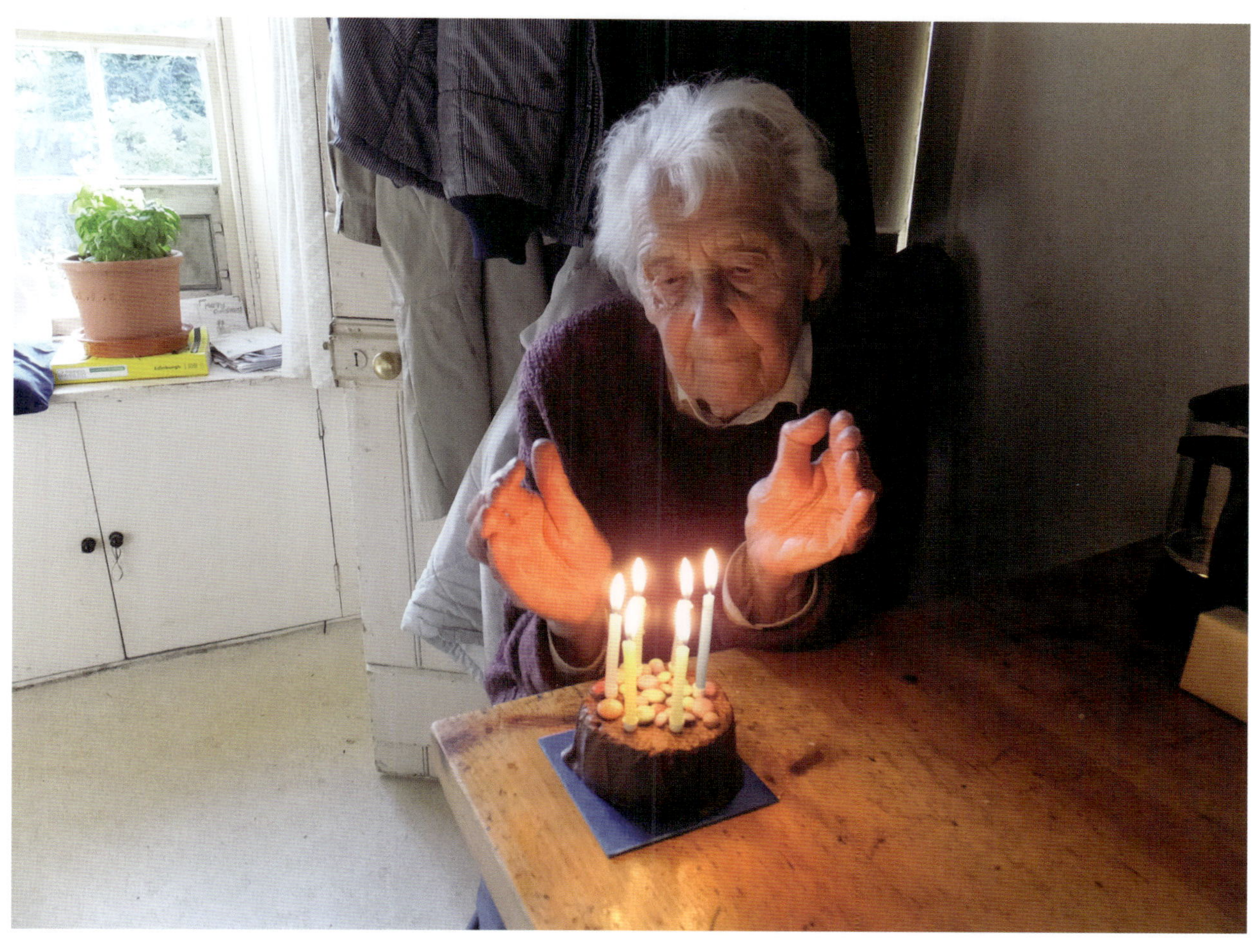

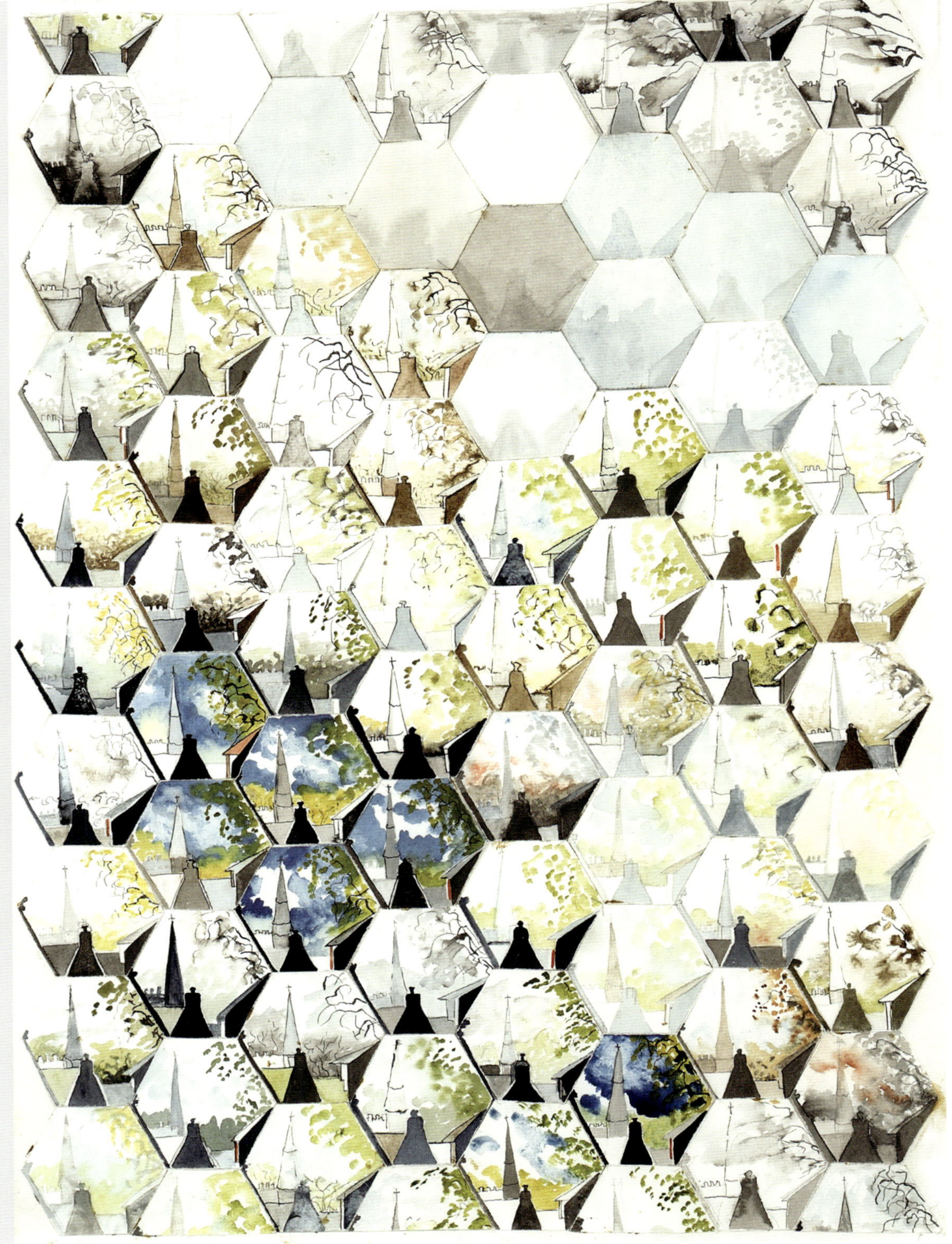